Teaching Poor Readers in the Secondary School

CHRISTINE CASSELL

CROOM HELM
London & Canberra

© 1982 Christine Cassell
Croom Helm Ltd, 2 – 10 St John's Road, London SW11

British Library Cataloguing in Publication Data

Cassell, Christine
   Teaching poor readers in the secondary school.
   — (Croom Helm special education series)
   1. Reading (Secondary education)
   2. Reading — Remedial teaching
   3. Reading disability
   I. Title
   371.91′4   LB1632

ISBN 0-7099-0294-8

Typeset in Times on a Compugraphic Editwriter
by Pat Murphy Studios, Highcliffe-on-Sea, Dorset

Printed and bound in Great Britain
by Billing and Sons Limited
Guildford, London, Oxford, Worcester

Contents

Preface

This book is intended as a practical manual which will enable secondary teachers, whether or not they are specialist remedial teachers, to plan and organise a remedial programme for pupils still at the very beginning stages of learning to read. There already exists a large number of books on reading, covering research and theory, testing and teaching approaches. Many are too general to be of practical value, others too jargon-laden or wordy to be accessible to the non-specialist. In order to be usable by the working teacher the approach outlined here aims to be as practical and realistic as possible in terms of the demands on time, materials and knowledge of theory. However, some commitment of time is necessary if a reading programme is to be planned to meet the needs of individual pupils.

The emphasis throughout is on the task of reading itself, and how the task may be broken down into suitable learning steps for the child who has experienced prolonged difficulty in learning to read. The assessment procedure reflects this emphasis by concentrating on the child's current level of competence in reading rather than on skills and deficits in hypothetical abilities assumed to underlie the task. Assessment, programme design and record keeping are all closely linked, and based on the assumption that for a child who is experiencing difficulty, it is meaningful to analyse the reading task into a series of sub-goals or stages. A progression of stages based, in the absence of research evidence, on teaching experience and common sense is provided, although this is not intended as a rigid series of steps through which every child should pass. It is designed to provide a structure for the teacher, but one that can be modified to suit the learning rates, patterns and preferences of individual pupils. Such a structure helps both pupil and teacher to be aware of the long and short term goals of the reading programme and to monitor progress.

The book is divided into three sections. The first section outlines an assessment procedure, the second deals with the setting of long and short term goals of the programme, and the third section covers teaching methods and materials.

Assessment for Teaching

It is a sad fact that many children reach secondary school age as very poor readers.

Schools vary in the extent to which they help such children, but even in the most sympathetic schools they face enormous problems. Across the curriculum, secondary school work requires some competence in reading and writing. The child with little or no reading finds it difficult to make progress in any subject and is doomed to general failure in school. As this follows on from the failure already experienced at the junior school it is not surprising that behaviour problems are often associated with reading problems at the secondary level. Therefore, any fresh attempts to teach the child to read must be carefully planned to produce success that will be easily apparent to the child himself.

Selecting Poor Readers for the Programme

The first thing to do is to decide which children you intend to work with. As the programme is intended for non-readers and very poor readers many teachers will have a clear idea of the likely candidates in their class. The pupils who will benefit from this approach are those with reading ages of about eight years or below. There is considerable variation in the amount of information that different junior schools pass on to the secondary schools but there is usually at least some indication of a pupil's reading level. Where such information is lacking for an individual or for a group of children it may be necessary to administer some form of reading test.

There is a wide variety of individual and group reading tests available to the teacher. They vary in the task they set the pupil and therefore in the aspects of reading they assess. A group test which asks the pupil to read sentences silently and then fill in missing words measures a different skill from an individual test which requires the pupil to read aloud a series of unconnected words. Appendix A gives a list of reading tests suitable for children of secondary age indicating whether they are group or individual, and giving some idea of what the child has to do.

Since, at this stage, all that is required is a guide to a child's reading level to identify potential candidates for the programme, the nature of the test given is not particularly important. It is more important to have some idea of the reliability and meaning of the scores. Standardised tests vary in the accuracy with which they gauge an individual's standing on a particular test compared with the rest of the population. All tests have some degree of error which needs to be taken into account if you are to avoid overestimating or underestimating a child's reading level, or assuming that changes in test score are due to progress (or the opposite) when, in fact, they are due to the unreliability of the test. Some children's scores will be spuriously high, others spuriously low, because of this unreliability. Some of the well-standardised tests quote the 'standard error' of measurement for different age levels. For example, if the standard error of a test is given as 2.5 and a pupil obtains a score of 15, we can be 68 per cent certain that the pupil's true score falls between 12.5 and 17.5, i.e. between 15± the standard error. Such a discrepancy may make a difference of several months or even a year to the reading age, and a child's reading age should therefore only be quoted as falling within the range indicated. Where the standard error of a test is not provided, the reading age should be recognised as a rough estimate with an unspecified degree of error.

A reading test may be used to give an indication of a child's reading attainment relative to other children of his age, and to select poor readers in need of particular help, but it does not in itself provide a basis on which to design a teaching programme. Two children who obtain the same score on a reading test may have quite different teaching needs and respond quite differently to learning tasks. Recognition of this has led to the publication of an abundance of diagnostic batteries, many of which attempt to assess a child's strengths and weaknesses in a variety of hypothetical abilities with impressive-sounding names like visual discrimination, auditory sequential memory and figure-ground perception, which are assumed to underlie the ability to read. Whilst common sense supports the notion that visual and auditory discrimination are involved in the reading task, one is faced with the problem of knowing what minimum level of auditory or visual discrimination is necessary to learn to read, and how to measure it. There are indeed many poor readers who have difficulty in auditory or visual discrimination tasks, but also some competent readers who have such difficulties. Visual and auditory discrimination are therefore only important to the extent that they relate directly to the reading tasks encountered and the child's difficulties in coping with them. Rather than the teacher spending valuable time and effort in trying to develop auditory and visual 'skills', which may or may not generalise to the reading task, it is felt that with most children the subtleties of the process of learning to read, and their own individual needs, are best understood by focusing on the reading task itself. If you want to know whether a child will be able to learn to read by a particular teaching method, or with certain materials, it makes sense to try teaching by that method or with those materials and, if the child fails to learn, to adapt your teaching until it does suit the child's needs.

Focusing on the reading task itself also places greater value on the teacher's skills in assessment, and links the assessment to the teaching and the recording of progress that is to follow. The assessment schedule offered here reflects an attempt to analyse the task of learning to read into a series of steps. It does not claim to represent the stages through which *all* children progress. The way in which the majority of children learn to read has defied description, probably because each child approaches the task differently. Even if one could describe the progression and learning strategies used by children who come easily to the reading task, it could not be assumed that those who, for one reason or another, have failed to learn to read in the infant and junior school would follow the same route or use the same strategies.

The series of steps given here is based largely on teaching observation of the stages through which it has been useful to take failed readers. For some of the steps the order is important in that the acquisition of later ones does depend on, or is facilitated by, the acquisition of earlier ones, but for others the order is irrelevant.

Using the Assessment Schedule

Once the poor readers have been identified you are almost ready to begin looking in more detail at just what stage a child has reached. Before you do go on, however, it is important to check whether any of your poor readers might have undetected defects of hearing or eyesight: poor articulation (especially of consonants) is a clue to the first, direct questioning the simplest check on the second; remember that *near*-sightedness is not normally checked at school medicals.

The assessment schedule (Table 1, p. 5) is a checklist of steps, on each of which a pupil's competence can be evaluated. It is intended that the checklist should be reproduced by the teacher and used as a testing record. Explanatory notes and necessary word lists for assessing each step on the checklist follow. The assessment needs to be completed for each child you intend to work with and may be quite time-consuming, but as it is not a standardised procedure there are no strict rules about it being completed in one session under given conditions. There are a few general points that need to be borne in mind when using the assessment schedule but items may be administered individually when you are able to find the time. Pupils are more likely to try their best if what you are doing and why is explained to them. Reading tests of any kind will be all too familiar to these pupils as something at which they do very badly, and tact is therefore required. A child should understand that it does not matter if he does not know some of the words or gets some wrong, but that he should try them so that you will know how to set about helping him. Whether you have to find time outside of lessons to see a pupil alone depends very much on the organisation of the school and classroom. In classrooms where the teacher normally moves about sitting with different individuals or groups to mark or discuss their work, it is possible to ask a pupil to read some words during the lesson without causing embarrassment.

Table 1: Assessment Schedule

```
                              NAME .........................

                              D.O.B. .......................

                              AGE ...................
```

Does pupil:

1. read any words in the context of a familiar book? If less than 20

   list them ....

   ....

   ....

2. read any words out of context, for example on flashcards? If less than

   20 list them ....

   ....

   ....

3. recognise aurally the initial letter sound of words?

4. associate the initial sounds of words with the relevant letter symbols?
   Circle those not known.

   b   e   h   s   w   j   c   d   l   m   a

   f   g   i   r   n   p   q   o   v   u   t   y

5. read phonetically regular 3-letter words? Record errors.

mat	fan	top	log	kit	bin	fin	tot	leg	sit	ban
man	run	bus	beg	red	rug	pot	ran	but	big	rod
bug	lot	tin	bed	hot	van	rag	lid

6. read phonetically regular words beginning with consonant blends?
   Record errors.

blot	clap	flop	glad	slot	brag	crop	drip	from	pram
trap	scab	skid	snap	smell	swim	twig	grip	scrub
plan	clip	flag	frog	slam	trot

7. read the following words containing consonant pairs? Record errors.

   stop   quit   chat   west   step   chip   lost   quest   shot

   wish   fish   shin

8. read phonetically regular 4-letter words ending in two consonants?
   Record errors.

   bell   duck   sent   help   mend   held   camp   sell   sock

   bent   gulp   band   wild   limp   pill

9. read words with common endings? Record errors.

   lets   topple   running   camped   sits   sitting   wobble

   wishing   fished   apple   stops   helped.

10. read words containing <u>oo</u> or <u>ee</u>? Record errors.

    keep   book   loop   feed   hook   peel   roof   weep

11. read phonetically regular words containing vowel/consonant
    combinations? Record errors.

    raid   hard   launch   claw   hawk   away   sway   meat   jerk

    term   bread   chew   field   seize   bird   third   boat   boil

    toad   port . trout   mouse   cow   frown   toy   snow   flown

    hurt   turn   joy

12. read words in which the vowel sound is modified by the final letter
    'e' ? Record errors.

    came   time   home   tube   line   sane   cube   robe   rude

    side   pole   wade

13. read words of two or more syllables? Record errors.

    window   carpet   garden   sunset   rainbow   bookcase   hotter

    after   happiness   unlucky   disgusting   decorate   holiday

    episode   footballer   recorder

14. read words with -ion or -ious endings? Record errors.

   ration   victorious   station   occasion   ambitious   intrusion

   glorious   relation   competition   fictitious   abrasion   donation

15. use contextual cues in reading?

   Yes.......   No ....   Observations ....

   ....

16. answer questions on material read with 99% accuracy?

   Record number of correct and incorrect answers:

   Correct ....   Incorrect ....

17. Trial teaching:

   Words read at the end of session 1 ....

   ....

   ....

   Words read at the end of session 2 ....

   ....

   ....

   Words read at the end of session 3 ....

   ....

   ....

NOTES

Figure 1: Pictures for Assessment Item 3

Procedure

(1)   These first two items are intended for the very poorest readers who can
and   read a few words only. Many of the children being assessed on this
(2)   schedule will be able to read well over 20 words, and you will be aware
        that they can, either from experience of teaching them or from their
        performance on a reading test. For children who you know or suspect
        can read only a few words it is important to find out what these words are
        and just how many. Obviously it is not possible to provide a word list
        suitable to test these two items. If a child can read only three words it is
        pointless and demoralising to let him plough through a long list,
        particularly as his three words may not be on it.
            The best way to discover what words a child can read is to find out
        what reading material he has been exposed to, and present some of this
        to see if he can recognise any of the words. If he can read some words in
        context, you can then write these on flashcards or pieces of paper to see if
        he can read them in isolation.

(3)   Present the pupil with the pictures on page 8 (Figure 1) and check that he
        is able to name each of them. Ask him to consider one row at a time and
        ask 'Which of these begins with the sound 'c'?' etc. Make the consonant
        sound as close as possible to its sound in the word without actually
        adding a vowel sound.
            This item is concerned with whether the pupil can attend to, and
        aurally isolate, the initial sound of words which seems to be a necessary
        preliminary to learning to associate particular sounds with letter
        symbols. Separating the initial sound may seem an artifical activity,
        particularly as the initial consonant sound is modified by the following
        vowel and cannot really be articulated without an adjoining vowel, but it
        shows whether the child will be able to associate initial letter sounds and
        symbols which is a useful aid to word recognition.

(4)   Present the pupil with the letters on pages 10 – 12 (Figure 2). Expose one
        line at a time, and ask 'Which letter comes at the beginning of ......?' Use
        the following words:

EGG	HOUSE	BOTTLE	SUN	WINDOW	APPLE
JET	CAR	DOG	LETTER	MOUSE	PAPER
FOG	GARDEN	INK	RECORD	NEEDLE	YELLOW
QUEEN	ORANGE	VEST	UMBRELLA	TABLE	

The aim is to find out whether the pupil has begun to learn initial letter
sounds, and identify those known and those not known.

Figure 2

b   e   h   s   w

a   d   c   l   j   m   Letters for Assessment Item 4

f   g   i   n   p   r

t   u   q   o   v   y

mat	fan	top	log	kit	bin	
fin	tot	leg	sit	ban	man	
run	bus	beg	red	rug	pot	Words for Item 5
ran	but	big	rod	bug	lot	
tin	bed	hot	van	rag	lid	

blot	clap	flop	glad	slot	
brag	crop	drip	from	pram	
trap	scab	skid	snap	smell	Words for Item 6
swim	twig	grip	scrub	plan	
clip	flag	frog	slam	trot	

stop	quit	chat	west	
step	chip	lost	quest	Words for Item 7
shot	wish	fish	shin	

bell	duck	sent	help	mend
held	camp	sell	sock	bent
gulp	band	wild	limp	pill

Words for Item 8

lets	topple	running	camped
sits	sitting	wobble	wishing
fished	apple	stops	helped

Words for Item 9

keep	book	loop	feed
hook	peel	roof	weep

Words for Item 10

raid	hard	launch	claw	hawk
away	sway	meat	jerk	term
bread	chew	field	seize	bird
third	boat	boil	toad	port
trout	mouse	cow	frown	toy
snow	flown	hurt	turn	joy

Words for Item 11

came	time	home	tube
line	sane	cube	robe
rude	side	pole	wade

Words for Item 12

window	carpet	garden	sunset
rainbow	bookcase	hotter	after
happiness	unlucky	disgusting	decorate
holiday	episode	footballer	recorder

Words for Item 13

ration	victorious	station	occasion
ambitious	intrusion	glorious	relation
competition	fictitious	abrasion	donation

Words for Item 14

(5)   The purpose of this item is to discover whether a child can use phonic cues to help him read phonetically-regular 3-letter words. Some such words may have been learnt by sight so it is necessary to ask him to read a selection, including some less common ones. The list of words given for this item (p. 10) should allow you to decide whether he can consistently use phonic cues to read 3-letter words.

You need not ask the child to read all the words given; if it is clear that he cannot read them at all you can stop after three or four words. With children who know some of the words, and make a reasonable attempt at others, try to find out why certain words present difficulty. Is the child, as is common at this stage, confusing some of the medial vowel sounds? Is he paying attention to the final consonant sound? Does he say the sounds aloud but then find it impossible to blend the sounds into a word? Record any errors and your observations. More detailed questions about a pupil's performance will come later, but it is useful to begin making observations at this stage.

(6) to (14)   These items test the pupil's ability to read words containing a variety of letter sounds, and those consisting of more than one syllable. Some letter combinations are generally assumed to be more difficult to learn than others, and many phonic teaching schemes recommend similar if not identical sequences for introducing sounds. The order of these assessment items reflects the order used in a number of phonic schemes and therefore the order in which many children will have been taught sounds. However, children may know some of the sounds in later assessment items but not those in earlier ones, either because they have had no

phonic teaching and therefore acquired knowledge of letter sounds incidentally and haphazardly, or because they have learnt and retained only some parts of the teaching programme. A pupil may therefore not know any of the words in (8) yet be able to read those for (10).

In general you should discontinue an item once the child has failed on three consecutive words, unless he is very keen to go on. There will come a point with many pupils where it is clear that they will not be able to read any words of later items, and rather than set down rigid rules as to when to stop testing, this is left to the teacher's discretion, as it is important not to undermine a pupil's confidence by continuing too long past the point of failure.

(15) If the child is able to read sentences or short passages you can begin to look at the reading strategies employed, and one important question to ask is whether the child is using *contextual cues*.

Present the pupil with a short passage (four to five sentences) in which there are a few words (no more than one per sentence) that he does not know. Observe and record the attempts the pupil makes at the unknown words. Does he guess wildly, use phonic cues to work out the word, guess the word from the meaning of the sentence — or seem to use some combination of these strategies? If he is using the sense of the sentence to discover the unknown word, is the word he suggests the right part of speech and does it have the right meaning?

(16) Present the pupil with a passage which he can read with no less than 99 per cent accuracy. You may need to ask him to read it aloud to ensure that he does know all the words, but allow him also to read it through silently as the effort of reading aloud may interfere with comprehension. Remove the passage and ask several questions about its content. The questions should require the pupil to have fully understood what he has read and it should not be possible for him just to repeat a phrase or sentence from the passage as an answer.

Trial Teaching

The assessment schedule has now been completed providing a record of the sorts of words the pupil is able to read as well as some idea of the strategies he uses in reading. At this point it is useful to try to teach the pupil some of the words he was unable to read. This will give an indication of how large or small the steps of your programme will need to be, and how much repetition and reinforcement will be necessary for each stage. It will make easier the planning of short and long term objectives described in the next section.

Choose five words he is unable to read, but which it is reasonable to expect him to learn. For the pupil who knows few or no words, select five common nouns that look and sound fairly different and that it would be useful for him to know (see ESA First Words Cards, p. 54). For the pupil who can use some phonic cues in reading, choose five words containing a letter combination whose sound he seems not yet to know (e.g. 'ai' as in 'hair', 'chair', 'stairs', etc.).

Spend about ten minutes teaching the words, by saying them as you point to them, asking the pupil to repeat the words after you and perhaps write them down, and by drawing attention to various features of the words such as initial letter sound and length. At the end of the session record which words the pupil can and cannot read. Test him again on these same words half an hour later (or some time later the same day) and again the following day. If some words previously learnt have been forgotten, provide some clues to find out how much help is needed before the word is remembered. If there were words still unlearnt at the end of the first session try these again; perhaps they will be more easily learnt on the second or third occasion.

The purpose of these trial teaching sessions is to give an indication of the number of words you should work on at a time and how much repetition will be needed before they are remembered. Such sessions are particularly useful with pupils you do not know very well, but you may find that you are surprised by pupils who have been teaching for some time. Someone who appears to have a good general knowledge, is articulate and able to reason well during class discussions may have a lot of difficulty remembering words under these circumstances, whereas another child you would not expect it of learns the words quite easily. In some cases you will decide that five is the maximum number of words you would want to introduce at a time, in other cases you may feel that the pupil could deal with at least ten.

Summary

Chapter 1 covers the initial stages of planning a teaching programme and enables you to:

(1) Select pupils for your programme.
(2) Carry out and record initial assessment.
(3) Carry out and record trial teaching sessions.

CHAPTER 2

Planning the Programme

Having completed the assessment schedule and trial teaching, the next step is to plan the programme to meet the pupil's needs, bearing in mind his present reading ability, the reading demands made on him by the curriculum he follows and what it would be most immediately useful for him to know, written as a sequence of clearly stated learning objectives. The emphasis should be on what the pupil can do at the moment, and what you would like him to be able to do as a result of your teaching.

The learning objectives approach advocated here concentrates on the features of the situation which are relatively easy to change, namely teaching content, methods and materials, rather than 'intelligence', 'home background' and so on. Schools cannot change their pupils' background, though parents' support in any remedial programme is useful, but they can significantly affect attainment, and influence behaviour both in and out of school. The assumptions are that the child *can* learn, and that the teacher has the skills, and has or can acquire the techniques to teach him.

Setting the Main Goals

Setting main goals means being realistic: defining your goals for the next two terms as something within the pupil's reach, but not so well within his reach that you are restricting progress. The results of the assessment and trial teaching should help you to define goals which it is reasonable to assume the pupil could attain within a few months. A child who has learnt ten new words on the trial teaching can be set a far more ambitious goal than a child who has retained only one word with difficulty. Consideration of the areas of the curriculum where the pupil experiences most difficulty should help to select teaching priorities.

But where do you start, and how do you define your goals? The assessment schedule concentrates largely on two approaches to teaching reading: the teaching of words 'by sight', and the teaching of words grouped according to phonic rules. This is not the only way to break down the reading process for teaching, but the author has found, as have others involved in teaching reading to secondary-age pupils, that it is an effective approach. We shall return to this issue of how one breaks down the task for teaching when we consider the detailed planning of the remedial programme, but at this stage the main goals of the programme can be defined in terms of *sight vocabulary, ability to read phonetically regular words* and *reading for meaning*.

You may find, using the assessment schedule with a pupil, that he can read only five words out of context. An appropriate aim for this child would be to teach him a basic sight vocabulary. Sight vocabulary refers to words which the pupil can read without necessarily knowing or using the letter-sound relationships involved. Because he is not expected to work out the words by phonic rules, it is possible to introduce irregular words, and words containing the more complex letter-sound relationships in the early stages, and thus include words which are useful and of interest to the pupil.

The trial teaching sessions will help to determine how many words to include in that target sight vocabulary. Let us assume that the child could recall all ten words after 30 minutes, but only four words a day later. It would seem reasonable to expect him to be able to learn ten new words in a week, and therefore to set 100 words as the target for the term. What those 100 words are is a matter for negotiation between the teacher and the pupil. It is necessary to bear in mind the age and interests of the pupil, the curriculum he follows, and the materials available. If a boy has a hobby or interest that occupies much of his spare time then he may well be motivated to learn words associated with that hobby. Knowing just one or two words may enable him to read the labels on the fishing tackle he is buying, or to read some of the specifications of the machines in his motorcycle magazine. Words which crop up frequently in lessons can be included in the sight vocabulary as well as the common 'key' words such as 'the', 'are', 'and', etc. (A list of key words is given in Table 2.) If there is a reading scheme or series of books at a suitably simple level (see Appendix B) to which the pupil is attracted, the vocabulary from that can be part of the target.

The child who could read only five words out of context may also know only one or two letter sounds. Teaching of the letter sound/letter symbol associations could therefore become a parallel aim to teaching a sight vocabulary. The aims for such a pupil would therefore be:
— to teach a basic sight vocabulary,
— to teach the association between the sounds at the *beginning* of words and their symbols.

Another child might have quite a large sight vocabulary yet stumble over unfamiliar phonetically-regular words containing certain letter combinations. The broad aim for this pupil might be:
— to teach phonic word attack.

Other pupils may be quite competent in the mechanical aspects of reading, that is they may be able to make the right noises when they see the printed word on the page, but not understand adequately the meaning of what they are reading. The ability to use contextual cues is related to ability to read for meaning. The competent reader relies heavily on semantic and syntactic cues, paying little

Table 2: Common Words in Written English

Twelve words make up, on average, a quarter of all reading material:

a	and	he	I	in	is	it	of	that	the	to	was

The following twenty words, together with the twelve given above, account for about one third of all reading matter:

all	as	at	be	but	are	for	had	have	him	his	not
on	one	said	so	they	we	with	you				

The following sixty-eight words combine with the above thirty-two words to comprise, on average, one half of all reading material:

about	an	back	been	before	big	by	call	came	can	come
could	did	do	down	first	from	get	go	has	her	here	if
into	just	like	little	look	made	make	more	me	much	must
my	no	new	now	off	old	only	or	our	other	out	over
right	see	she	some	their	them	then	there	this	two	up
want	well	went	were	what	when	where	which	who	will
your

The hundred next most used words:

after	again	always	am	another	any	ask	away	bad	because
best	bird	black	blue	boy	bring	day	dog	don't	eat	every
far	fast	father	fell	find	five	fly	four	found	gave	girl
give	going	good	got	green	hand	have	head	help	home
house	how	jump	keep	know	last	left	let	live	long	man
many	may	men	mother	Mr.	never	next	once	open	own
play	put	ran	read	red	room	round	run	sat	saw	say
school	should	sing	sit	soon	stop	take	tell	than	these
thing	think	three	time	too	tree	under	us	very	walk	white
why	wish	work	would	year

Fifty additional nouns:

apple	baby	bag	ball	bed	book	box	bus	car	cat	children
cow	cup	dinner	doll	door	egg	end	farm	fish	fun	hat
hill	horse	jam	letter	milk	money	morning	Mrs.	name	night
nothing	picture	pig	place	rabbit	road	sea	shop	sister	street
sun	table	tea	today	top	toy	train	water

These 250 words make up approximately 70 per cent of juvenile reading and about 60 per cent of adult reading.

Source: J. McNally and W. Murray, *Keywords to Literacy* (Schoolmaster Publ. Co., London, 1964).

attention to individual words and letters except when meeting a totally unfamiliar word when it may be necessary to resort to a phonic analysis. This is borne out by the difficulty we, as skilled readers, experience in attempting to proof read a passage for typing or spelling errors. Somehow children must progress from the word-by-word recognition prevalent in the learning stages to more fluent reading where the text is sampled and predictions about subsequent words made on the basis of the reader's knowledge of the rules of language. An early emphasis on *reading for meaning* seems to aid this transition and make clear the purpose of the learning task. Therefore, aims such as:

— to teach the use of contextual cues,
— to teach the pupil to read for meaning,
should also be considered.

Although it is possible to find a number of goals appropriate to each pupil, it is a good idea initially to restrict them to two main priorities. Having chosen these main goals; *write them down!* This may seem unnecessary, particularly if you are dealing with only one pupil, as you may feel that you could remember them well enough. But the clear stating and recording of aims and objectives is crucial to this approach. Proper evaluation and modification of the programme as it progresses cannot take place without it.

The Detailed Planning

Stating the broad aims of the programme is just the beginning. Further thought must now be given to the steps necessary to achieve those aims.

A child who has reached the secondary school without learning to read effectively has experienced a great deal of failure. He will probably lack confidence in approaching any reading task, have a poor self-image and have come to dislike reading intensely as something at which he cannot succeed. He has perhaps begun to avoid the thing at which he fails by clowning or misbehaving in class, and found this a rewarding alternative to work if it produces admiration from his peers and plenty of attention from the teachers, taking the focus *off* his reading.

For these reasons. it is essential that new attempts to teach a child at secondary level do not allow him to fail. This means designing a carefully graded programme which ensures that the pupil is learning and moving towards the goal in steps he can master. Each step of such a programme must be stated clearly so that both pupil and teacher can see that it has been mastered before moving on to the next step. These clear statements of the steps leading to the teaching goal, which we shall refer to as the *objectives* of the programme, provide the details of the remediation, specifying just what one expects a pupil to be able to do as a result of teaching.

An objective describes an *action* which the pupil can be *observed* doing. The following are examples of such *behavioural* objectives:
— pupil matches the words 'tree', 'house', 'table' and 'window' to appropriate pictures.
— pupil reads the words 'tree', 'house', 'window' and 'table' on flashcards.
— pupil groups pictures of objects according to initial letter sound.
This reference to *pupil* behaviour is most important. It is easy to refer to teacher behaviour, to describe what has been taught (this child has been through the XYZ programme, etc.) and assume that this can be equated with

what has been learnt. Shifting attention to the pupil means concerning ourselves with observable behaviours. If the pupil is expected to know the words 'tree', 'house', 'table' and 'window', we have to determine how we will know whether this has been achieved — what is our criterion of knowing — and therefore in writing behavioural objectives we should specify just what we expect the pupil to be able to *do* as a result of our teaching.

Since the programme is for pupils who do not easily learn things spontaneously, we need to write objectives for each of the things we want them to learn on the way to attaining the ultimate goal. Breaking the aim|or goal into suitable objectives involves analysis of the task being taught. Task analysis attempts to describe the steps a learner may need to go through in mastering the task, which may be anything from putting on a vest to using calculus. Essentially this is nothing new; it is simply what teachers spend much of their time doing and is usually quite straightforward. But for a child having difficulty learning a task this process needs to be more clearly defined and the task more rigorously broken down into component steps. For example, if you attempt to write down the steps involved in even a simple task you begin to see that there could be a number of alternative routes. Three teachers wrote these task analyses for sorting shapes:

(1) sorts circles, triangles, squares and rectangles of same colour according to shape.
(2) sorts circles, triangles, squares and rectangles of different colours according to shape.

(1) given two circles, two triangles, two squares and two rectangles of same colour matches shapes.
(2) given two circles, two triangles, two squares and two rectangles of assorted colours matches shapes.
(3) sorts pile of circles, triangles, squares and rectangles according to shape when of same colour.
(4) sorts pile of circles, triangles, squares and rectangles according to shape when of assorted colours.

(1) given circles and squares of same colour matches shapes.
(2) given triangles and rectangles of same colour matches shapes.
(3) given circles and triangles of same colour matches shapes.
(4) given squares and rectangles of same colour matches shapes.
(5) given circles, squares, triangles and rectangles, matches for shape.
(6) given circles and squares of assorted colours, matches for shape.
(7) given triangles and rectangles of assorted colours, matches for shape.
(8) given circles and triangles of assorted colours, matches for shape.
(9) given squares and rectangles of assorted colours, matches for shape.
(10) given circles, squares, triangles and rectangles of assorted colours, matches for shape.

As you can see, for a relatively simple task there is a range of possible task analyses. Each individual teacher had a particular child in mind and, as you will have gathered, the children were of quite different ages and ability. The last of the three was written for a child who the teacher knew would learn only slowly and who would not generalise from one discrimination task to another; having learnt to discriminate circles from squares and triangles from rectangles, the teacher was aware that this child would also need to learn to discriminate circles from triangles and squares from rectangles. So the analysis one writes for a task will depend both on the *task* and the *person to be taught*. The child's personality, ability and current level of competence in the task affect how finely the task needs to be broken down.

As well as the *number* of objectives, one must consider their *sequence* in a task analysis. Some steps will logically precede others, in that the learning of later steps may be dependent on, or be facilitated by, the learning of earlier ones. Consider the following sequence.

(1) matches letter symbols,
(2) groups pictures of objects according to initial letter sound,
(3) matches pictures to initial letter symbols.

Although it would be possible to teach objective (3) without going through (1) and (2), it seems likely that the learning of objectives (1) and (2) would help the pupil to learn to match pictures to the appropriate letter symbols. In other instances the order of objectives will be arbitrary. For example, in the sequence below, the order of learning the sounds is unimportant; the learning of one does not necessarily contribute to the learning of the others:

(1) reads phonetically regular words beginning with *sh* (e.g. ship, shop, shed),
(2) reads phonetically regular words beginning with *ch* (e.g. chop, chip, check),
(3) reads phonetically regular words beginning with *st* (e.g. stop, step, stick).

There are no simple rules to follow in writing a task analysis; it is not easy and can only be accomplished by giving careful thought to the task and the pupil to be taught. It may be helpful, however, to ask yourself the following questions when attempting to write a sequence of objectives for a given task:
What is the *target* behaviour?
What steps does the pupil need to master on the way to this objective?
Are the learning objectives placed in the order most likely to facilitate learning?
Ideally, one should, as a teacher, spend some time analysing the task to be taught to an individual or a group of pupils, then on the basis of this and the pupil's assessed level of competence, write a sequence of the objectives for teaching. But where does one begin in writing a task analysis for a skill as complex as reading? As we have already mentioned, research has failed to

provide a detailed description of the way in which children learn to read. There may be a number of *different* routes. The only thing we can say with any certainty is that some children find it very much more difficult than others. It is therefore not possible to write a *definitive* task analysis, but some guidelines as to how one might break down the task are given here, based on the author's experience of teaching reading to pupils who have known repeated failure, and that of many colleagues.

Some Guidelines Towards a Task Analysis of Reading

We have already suggested three broad areas into which the task may be divided, namely *sight vocabulary, phonic word attack* and *comprehension.* These areas will be considered separately.

Sight Vocabulary

As mentioned, it seems sensible, in teaching a pupil to read from scratch, to begin by teaching some meaningful sentences or phrases 'by sight'. The word 'sight' used here and in the phrase 'sight vocabulary' is somewhat misleading as it implies that the child learns just by looking. A number of terms — 'sight approach', 'look and say' and 'whole word method' — are used to describe a child's learning of words without building them from component sounds. In fact the distinction between sight and phonic approaches is often a false one as far as the pupil's learning is concerned and children presented with whole words from the beginning may use a number of cues, including initial letter, to discriminate between and remember words. Similarly, those taught by a phonic approach may not in fact build the words from the constituent sounds. The distinction between sight and phonic approaches is more usefully applied to the teaching method than the way children actually learn.

It seems important that children experience the success of reading meaningful units at the beginning of learning to read so that the task appears a sensible one, and the value of their learning is immediately apparent. If one of your main aims for a particular pupil is to teach him a sight vocabulary, you will by now have decided on the content of your target vocabulary for the term or next eight to ten weeks, and will have estimated the number of words you can expect him to learn in a week. Assuming that you intend to teach the ten words of the following sentences — 'Please complete in block letters. Return to the above address' — your programme plan may read as follows:

Main Goal: to teach a basic sight vocabulary.

Immediate Aim: to teach the words of the sentences — 'Please complete in block letters. Return to the above address.'

Objectives:
(1) pupil matches sentence cards
(2) pupil matches words given two flashcards of each
(3) pupil matches individual words to sentence cards
(4) pupil matches sentences to picture clues, and then reads sentences to teacher
(5) where appropriate, matches individual words to picture clues and then reads words to teacher
(6) assembles flashcards of individual words to form sentences
(7) given jumbled sentences writes them in correct word order
(8) reads sentences on flashcards without clues
(9) reads individual words on flashcards
(10) finds and reads the sentences on forms.

You will note that the child is required to complete a variety of simpler activities before finally being expected to read the sentences without clues. Most of the pupils you will be dealing with will need at least this many graded steps giving them plenty of experience of the words to be learned. The concept of 'overlearning' is a useful one. Overlearning refers to the repetition of a task beyond the point at which the child has attained success; so even if he reads a word correctly ten out of ten times, learning activities associated with that word are continued so that his response becomes more and more automatic. As part of this overlearning the word can be presented in a variety of contexts. Children who have difficulty learning to read often fail to generalise their learning — they can read a word if it occurs in the familiar context of a reading book, or even on a flashcard, but not, for example, if it appears on the classroom wall. Before finalising the details of your sight vocabulary objectives you will probably find it helpful to read the third section of the book on teaching methods and materials. The suggestions for activities given there will help you to define a series of objectives that lead the pupil gradually to the target behaviour.

A child cannot know in advance every word he is likely to come across and so needs techniques for reading words he has never met before. Two sorts of cues seem to be important both in the learning stages and once competence has been achieved. These are *phonic cues* and *contextual cues*.

Teaching Phonics

children of secondary age who have made a start with reading but
to have reached a plateau, a course in the use of phonic cues can give
ding spurt. Others do not make any sudden leaps, but benefit from
eir attention drawn to some of the consistent letter-sound relation-
ildren whose language is limited in structure and vocabulary are less

able to predict words on the basis of the meaning and grammatical structure of preceding words, and may need to rely heavily on phonic cues.

How then does one begin to teach a pupil about the consistent letter-sound relationships of English? How can we analyse the task? As already indicated, there is no one correct analysis for any task, and the extent to which the task needs to be broken down will depend on the pupil one is teaching. You may have your own preferred sequence for teaching phonics, but the following is offered as a guide.

A Sequence for Phonic Teaching. Although there are many irregular spellings in English, for the majority of words there is a reasonably consistent relationship between the sound of the spoken word and the letters used in the written word. However, the segments of sound into which we divide words are largely arbitrary, and we must learn to make the discriminations between sounds which are relevant to English and ignore the irrelevant ones. We learn to distinguish between the different sound patterns at the beginning of 'tap' and 'cat', but although an analysis of acoustic patterns would show that the sound patterns at the beginning of 'big' and 'bald' are different, we learn to ignore this difference because we represent both patterns with the same letter.

Obviously the child has to be able to discriminate letter-sounds before he can begin to associate those sounds with the appropriate letter symbols. So before we can expect a child to point to, or write the letter 'c' if we say words beginning with that sound, we must be sure that he can distinguish words beginning with 'c' from words beginning with other sounds. The assessment schedule will have indicated whether a child can associate letter sounds with their symbols, and if he cannot, item (3) of the schedule will give some idea of whether he can discriminate between different sounds at the beginning of words. If a pupil is not discriminating between initial letter sounds, then suitable objectives would be:
— pupil sorts pictures of nouns into groups according to initial letter sound,
— hearing an initial letter sound, pupil points to a picture of an object beginning with that sound.

Neither of these objectives refers to specific letters so it is assumed that all letter sounds are to be covered. It may be necessary, however, to break down the task even further for some pupils, concentrating at first on a few, or even just two, letters at a time. In this case, different sounding rather than similar sounding letters should be grouped.

Once a pupil can focus attention on the initial sounds of words and discriminate the different sounds, he can be taught to associate the sounds with their appropriate letter symbols. Again the size of the learning steps will depend on the individual. If you have discovered from the assessment schedule that the child knows most of the letter sounds, you may need to write only one objective:
— pupil points to initial letter of spoken words from an array of all 26 letters.

For children who know no letter-sound associations, and those whose learning rate is slow, smaller steps will be needed. The first estimate of the appropriate step size may be wrong, and it may be necessary to adjust the pace as you teach. For slower pupils, then, the programme may be as follows:
— matches pictures of nouns beginning with *c*, *m* and *b* to appropriate letter symbols,
— matches pictures of nouns beginning with *p*, *s* and *f* to appropriate letter symbols,
— matches pictures of nouns beginning with *a*, *t* and *n* to appropriate letter symbols,
   etc.

The question of how, having learnt individual letter sounds, children should be taught to read simple words composed of these letters, e.g. hop, pin, ten, has been a subject of much debate. The issue centres round the fact that if you say the individual letters of, for example, hop, h-o-p, they sound very little like the word, and it requires some mental leap, 'auditory synthesis', 'sound blending', call it what you will, to realise that they make the word 'hop'.

Details of methods and materials will be left to Chapter 3, but obviously the approach you adopt will affect the objectives you write.

Many children find it very difficult to decide what sound each letter represents, and then hold these sounds in memory while they decide what word the sounds would produce when blended together. It is often suggested that children should therefore learn to blend two of the sounds of 3-letter words and then add the third sound. There is one school of thought that dictates that children should be encouraged to blend the consonant and vowel sound first, e.g. ca, and then add the final consonant, ca-t. One argument in favour of this order of teaching is that the vowel modifies considerably the sound of the initial consonant, and therefore it is important that the pupil gets this part of the word right before adding the ending.

The alternative is to blend the vowel with the final consonant, e.g. -at, and then add the initial consonant, c-at. The advantage of this approach is that blending the vowel with the final consonant frequently produces a meaningful word, e.g. c-at, t-in, s-it, although, more often, it doesn't, e.g. p-ot, t-ug, f-un.

It is probably best to avoid as far as possible the problem of sound blending aloud, as some children find this a positive hindrance and cannot modify them to produce a meaningful word. 'Silent' worksheets can sometimes help here. Having learnt individual letter sounds it may be sufficient for a pupil to learn groups of words containing similar letter patterns. For example, a pupil may learn 'cat' and, with his attention drawn to the similar endings and different initial letter sounds, then be able to read 'rat', 'hat', 'fat', 'sat'. Different approaches can be tried to find which teaching method suits a particular child. If he does need to build words by first producing the individual sounds, it is essential that he progresses to building words silently and finally to the stage where the majority of common words composed of sounds he has learned are read as quickly as sight words. Until he reaches this stage his reading will be faltering and lack fluency: he will be paying so much attention to the mechanics of reading that he is unlikely to be extracting much meaning.

When teaching 3-letter blends it is advisable to introduce one medial vowel sound at a time and make sure that those words can be read with confidence, both on flashcards and in the context of a sentence, before introducing a new vowel. Begin by teaching the 'a' words: cat, hat, bag, ran, etc., before going on to the 'i' words: pig, pin, hit, bib, etc. When he has been taught two vowel sounds the pupil should be able to read words containing each sound from a jumbled list as well as on flashcards and in sentences. Consider the order in which you introduce the sounds: any new vowel sound should be as auditorially distinct from the one just learnt as possible. Avoid teaching 'i' and 'e' together as these seem to be the most readily confused vowels. The best sequence is as follows:

a i o e u

Even when introduced one at a time, many children will tend to confuse the medial vowels and so will need activities that encourage them to pay attention to, and discriminate between, the vowel sounds in the middle of the words (see p. 59). Pupils must be able to read simple 3-letter words confidently, without hesitation and without confusing the short vowel sounds before they can be introduced to the next stages of a phonic programme.

The stages following 3-letter blends are largely a matter of choice but the following order, which has been found to be successful, is offered as a guideline. It progresses from word endings and letter combinations where the sounds blend together, to the more complicated letter combinations where two or more letters come together to produce a completely new sound.

Consonant pairs at the ends of words:
-*ck* as in back, tick, suck
-*ll* as in sell, pill, bull (but not ball, wall, etc. where the vowel sound is modified)

Word endings:
-*ing* as in running, kicking, having (the rules for dropping the final 'e' or doubling the final consonant need to be pointed out)
-*ed* as in stopped, hoped (explain the effect of doubling the final consonant)
-*s* as in stops, cups, runs
-*es* as in classes, buses

Consonant blends at the ends of words:
-*nt* as in bent, went, hunt
-*lp* as in help, gulp
-*mp* as in bump, lump, camp
-*nd* as in hand, land, send
-*lt* as in belt, felt, wilt

-lk as in milk, silk, hulk
-ld as in wild, old, held
-nk as in sink, tank, bank
-sh as in fish, wish, cosh

Consonant blends at the beginnings of words:
tr- as in trap, trip, trot
br- as in brat, brick
cr- as in crack, crisp
dr- as in drip, drill
pr- as in pram, prop
fr- as in frog, Fred
gr- as in grab, grit
bl- as in black, blob
cl- as in clap, click
pl- as in plan, plot
fl- as in flat, flop
gl- as in glad, glum
sl- as in slot, slip
sc- as in scab, scar
sk- as in skin, skid
sm- as in smell, smack
sn- as in snap, sniff
sp- as in spot, spit
sh- as in shop, shed
sw- as in swim, swell
tw- as in twin, twig
scr- as in scrap, scrub
spr- as in sprat, sprint
qu- as in quilt, quack

Words containing the sound all:
all, ball, wall, tall, hall, fall, small

Words containing the consonant combinations ch, th, st:
ch- and *-ch* as in chip, rich
th- and *-th* as in thick, that, filth, with
st- and *-st* as in stop, step, rest, lost

Words containing the double vowels oo and ee:
oo as in shoot, loot, root, spoon
oo as in book, look, took, hood
ee as in keep, sleep, see, sheet

Words in which the middle vowel is modified by the final 'e' (magic 'e')
a - e as in came, game, late, stale
e - e as in Pete, here
i - e as in time, line, shine, file
o - e as in hole, vote, note, home
u - e as in rule, cube, cute

Polysyllabic words:
Words composed of two smaller words: in/side, foot/step, sheep/dog
Words composed of two phonetically regular syllables: mag/net, rob/in
Words composed of three or more syllables: lem/on/ade, cat/a/pult

Words in which two vowels or a vowel and a consonant combine to produce a new sound:
ai as in train, again, mail
ar as in art, car, dark, garden
au as in August, haunt
aw as in saw, dawn, hawk
ay as in say, today, stay
ea as in meat, cheat, steam
ea as in bread, ready, instead
er as in jerk, herb, stern
ew as in new, flew, chew
ie as in field, yield, priest
ei as in eight, freight, weigh
ir as in bird, third, girl
oa as in boat, goat, load
ie, ue, oe as in die, blue, foe
oi as in oil, boil, joint, avoid
or as in fork, storm, torch
ou as in out, trout, pound
ow as in cow, how, drown, crowd
ow as in crow, low, snow, pillow
oy as in toy, boy, destroy, enjoy
ur as in hurt, church, turnip

Words containing igh and ght:
-igh as in high, thigh, sigh
-ght as in fight, bright, ought, taught

More difficult word endings:
-tion as in station, nation
-sion as in television, revision
-ious as in religious, cautious
-ous as in famous, dangerous

Comprehension

In teaching phonics there is always the danger of concentrating on the word recognition aspects of reading when there is much more to reading than making the right noises when presented with individual words. The purpose of reading is to extract *meaning* and it is essential that teaching objectives at all stages take this into account. Just as in the initial learning of a sight vocabulary it is important that the child learns to read meaningful sentences right from the beginning, so it is important that he reads phonetically regular words, not just as word lists, but in meaningful prose. Pupils should be encouraged to predict words both on the basis of the grammatical structure of the sentence and its meaning. In the sentence 'John climbed the – – –' for example, we know from our intuitive knowledge of the grammatical structure what type of word will come next. We expect it to be a noun or an adjective, and a child will recognise this even though the formal terms 'noun' and 'adjective' may not be familiar to him. 'John climbed the mountain' will make sense to the child: 'John climbed the motoring' will not. We expect something like 'mountain', 'tree', 'hill', 'ladder' or 'stairs' to follow. A child who could not read the word 'mountain' or the sounds 'ou' and 'ai' might yet accurately guess the word from the initial letter and contextual cues.

Activities which help children to make use of contextual cues are to be found in Chapter 3. They are not listed separately but are included in the sections on sight vocabulary and phonics, because our central purpose in teaching decoding skills is that they should be used to extract meaning from written material.

The Programme in Progress

Record Keeping

Records need to be kept so that a pupil's progress can be evaluated at any stage of the programme and modifications made where necessary. But record keeping should be an aid to teaching and the pupil's learning, not an end in itself. Pages of detailed notes take up too much of a busy teacher's time, are unlikely to be read by anyone and are of little value in the management of a reading programme. The main need is for a list of objectives with space to record when each is started and mastered. Once you have moved on to later objectives you will want, at intervals, to check that earlier ones are retained (especially where you have a sequence of different skills), so it is useful to have several 'check' columns to record the dates on which they are re-tested. Figure 3 is an example of a simple record sheet incorporating these points.

The objectives can be listed during the planning of the programme, leaving

Figure 3: A Simple Record Sheet

Goal			Name	
Objectives	Date Started	Date Mastered	Date Checked	Date Checked
1.				
2.				
3.				

only dates to be entered in the relevant columns during teaching. You may wish to add brief comments either in an additional column or on a separate sheet. Design your record sheet so that it fits into your mark book or a folder so you can carry it to different lessons and keep it up to date.

Modifying the Programme

Be prepared to modify the programme at any stage. The problems most likely to arise are ones of *step size*. If the step size chosen is too small you will find yourself organising more activities and materials than are necessary. The pupil will be mastering objectives very rapidly without the need for much repetition, and probably becoming bored with the pace of work. If, on the other hand, your steps are too large, the pupil will be spending a great deal of time on one objective, becoming bored as you struggle to find sufficient variety of material to cover this one point. As a rough guide, aim for objectives that can be mastered in one week, or even less than one week at the beginning of the programme. It is better, especially to start with, to have your steps a little too small than too big. Be prepared to keep changing the step size as you go; reduce it if particular words or sounds prove difficult or if motivation is flagging, increase it when progress is fast.

Calling in Outside Help

Although the suggestions put forward in this book aim to help you deal effectively and independently with specific cases, with pupils of secondary age who are this poor at reading, all help is welcome. Whether you are able to enlist the support of any education services outside the school in dealing with an individual or group of pupils will depend on the services available in your area and the demands being made on them. Many local authorities have remedial services that offer teaching to certain pupils or advice to teachers. Where specialist teachers do offer tuition it is often restricted to those pupils whose difficulties are specific to reading (children sometimes described as 'dyslexic'). The pupils you are teaching may be eligible for extra help although it is unlikely to be for more than one hour a week and they will still need all the help you can give them in school. If specialist teaching is provided you should liaise with the remedial teacher to make sure that your approaches are compatible.

Where extra teaching is not available you may be able to obtain advice from a *Remedial Advisory Service* or from the *Schools Psychological Service*. Many psychologists would be willing to discuss plans for helping an individual or group of pupils without your formally referring the child(ren). If you are able to make this kind of informal contact with the School Psychological Service you will be able to discuss whether, and at what point, a child should be referred formally.

Case Study

This case study is presented to illustrate the stages involved in the planning of a programme.

Michael had almost reached the end of his fourth year at comprehensive school barely able to read or write. His reading age on the *Burt Word Recognition Test* was about 8 years, and his own name was all he could write without copying. He was in the bottom of the three ability bands into which the school is organised, taking only non-examination courses. In all lessons except one, Michael was very quiet and unforthcoming, seeming to want, as his form-teacher put it, 'to fade into the background'. Although individually a pleasant lad, presenting no real behaviour difficulties, he had become a member of the breaktime smoking-in-the-toilets club, which had led to several negative encounters with members of staff. The only lesson in which Michael was talkative was motor mechanics. In this subject he would also make great efforts to write to complete his maintenance record sheet.

Michael had been referred to an educational psychologist in his junior school and again in his third year at secondary school. The psychologist described Michael as of 'limited intellectual potential' and recommended that an individual remedial programme be planned. A remedial programme covering some aspects of phonic word attack and vocabulary from the Adult Literacy Scheme had been attempted, but with limited success. Towards the end of Michael's fourth year his English and remedial teachers decided that they should limit their aims for his final year, structuring the programme more carefully, and therefore welcomed the approach described in this book when it was suggested. Michael's English teacher discussed their plan with him and completed the assessment schedule in two separate sessions. Michael enjoyed the individual attention of the assessment, and after the first session kept asking when the second would take place.

The Assessment

As can be seen from the completed assessment sheet, Michael knew a number of words both in a familiar context (a workcard on lorry driving) and on flash-cards, but, although he could read a range of phonetically regular words, he made errors even on the simple three-letter blends. He made good use of contextual cues in reading a passage, understanding material he could decode easily and even made an effort to make sense of material that was clearly beyond him.

Trial Teaching

Five phonetically regular words containing sounds on which Michael had made errors during assessment were chosen for the trial teaching session. During a 15 minute session Michael's teacher talked about the letter and sounds of the words and read them to him before Michael attempted reading and writing them. At the end of the session he could read the five words, in any order, without error.

The procedure was repeated over the next two days with five new words. As all the words were retained on the fourth day Michael's teacher felt it would be realistic to aim to teach about ten new words each week.

The Programme Plan

The areas that might be covered by the programme were discussed with Michael, and as his teachers had expected, he was keen to learn words associated with motor mechanics so that he could read some of the diagrams in the course manual. One main aim of the programme was therefore to teach a sight vocabulary including words from his motor mechanics manual as well as socially useful words and the 32 most common 'key' words (see Table 2). Although Michael recognised some of the 32 key words when tested on them, he was sufficiently unsure of them for all to be included for teaching.

Aim 1: to teach a sight vocabulary of the following words:
carburettor, engine, clutch, air filter, clean, cleaning, oil, brakes, needs, put, plugs
name, address, toilets, men, ladies, tickets, buses, station
a, and, he, I, in, is, it, of, that, the, to, was, all, as, at, be, but, are, for, had, have, him, his, not, on, one, said, so, they, we, with, you

Objectives:
(1) reads the sentences 'The carburettor needs cleaning. The air filter is clean' without picture clues.
(2) reads the words from the above sentences from flashcards, in any order, without error, on two consecutive days.
(3) accurately copies the above sentences from a card on his desk.
(4) reads the sentences 'The engine needs oil so I put it in. I clean all the plugs' without picture clues.
(5) reads the words from the above sentences from flashcards, in any order, without error, on two consecutive days.
(6) accurately copies the above two sentences from a card on his desk.
(7) reads accurately the four sentences taught so far when presented in any order.

A parallel aim, it was decided, would be to improve Michael's phonic word attack, beginning with 3-letter blends and common word endings. As he could already read the majority of 3-letter words, his teachers were looking to improve accuracy and speed of recognition so the first objectives here are not so finely graded as they are for sight vocabulary.

Aim 2: to improve phonic word attack.

Objectives:
(1) reads any phonetically regular word without error.
(2) reads any phonetically regular word without error within 2 seconds of presentation.

Figure 4: Assessment Schedule Completed for Case Study

NAME ..Michael...Brown.....

D.O.B. ....9. 11. 64............

AGE .15 y. 7 m..

Does pupil:

1. read any words in the context of a familiar book?   If less than 20

   list them ....20+...

   ....

   ....

2. read any words out of context, for example on flashcards?   If less

   than 20 list them ....20 +...

   ....

   ....

3. recognise aurally the initial letter sound of words?

   ✓

4. associate the initial sounds of words with the relevant letter

   symbols?   Circle those not known.

   b   e   h   s   w   j   c   d   l   m   a

   f   g   i   r   n   p   q   o   v   u   t   y
                          ✓

5. read phonetically regular 3-letter words?   Record errors.

       fot

   mat   fan   top   log   kit   bin   fin   tot   leg   sit   ban

   man   run   bus   beg   red   rug   pot   ran   but   big   rod

   bug   lot   tin   bed   hot   van   rig   lid
                                          rag

6. read phonetically regular words beginning with consonant blends?

   Record errors.

   blot   clap   flop   glad   slot   brag   crop   drip   from   pram

   trap   scab   skid   snap   smell   swim   grip   twig   scrub
                                  small

   plan   clip   flag   frog   slam   trot

7. read the following words containing consonant pairs?   Record errors.

stop   quit   chat   west   step   chip   lost   ~~quest~~   shot

wish   fish   shin

8. read phonetically regular 4-letter words ending in two consonants?
Record errors.

bell   duck   sent   help   mend   camp   sell   sock

bent   ~~gulp~~   band   wild   limp   pill

9. read words with common endings?   Record errors.

lets   topple   running   camped   sits   sitting   wobble

wishing   fished *fish*   apple   stops   helped

10. read words containing <u>oo</u> or <u>ee</u>?   Record errors.

keep   book   loop   feed   hook   peel   root   weep
                              ✓

11. read phonetically regular words containing vowel/consonant

combinations?   Record errors.

raid   hard   ~~launch~~   claw   hawk   away   sway   meat   jerk

term   bread   ~~chew~~   field   seize *size*   bird   third   boat   boil

~~toad~~   port   trout *trot*   ~~mouse~~   cow   frown   toy   snow   flown

hurt   turn   joy

12. read words in which the vowel sound is modified by the final letter

'e'?   Record errors.

came *com*   time   home   tube *tub*   line   sane   ~~cube~~   robe   ~~ride~~

side   pole   wade

13. read words of two or more syllables?   Record errors.

window   carpet   garden   sunset   rainbow   bookcase   hotter

after   happiness *happans*   unlucky   disgusting   decorate   holiday

~~episode~~   footballer   recorder

14. read words with -ion or -ious endings? Record errors.

~~ration~~ ~~victorious~~ station ~~occasion~~ ~~ambitious~~ ~~intrusion~~

~~glorious~~ ~~relation~~ ~~competition~~ ~~fictitious~~ ~~abrasion~~ ~~donation~~

15. use contextual cues in reading?

Yes ..✓.... No .... Observations ....

....

16. Answer questions on material read with 99% accuracy?

Record number of correct and incorrect answers:

Correct ......*5*......... Incorrect ....l..........

17. Trial teaching:

Words read at the end of session 1 ..tube...rude,..cube,.came,
..rule,.cute...

....

Words read at the end of session 2 ..tube..rude,..cube,.came,
..rule,.cute...

....

Words read at the end of session 3 ..tube,.rude,.cube,.came,
..rule,.cute...

NOTES

CHAPTER 3

Methods and Materials

Let us now assume that the aims and objectives of your programme are clearly defined and that you are ready to plan organisation of your teaching sessions.

Organising the Teaching Sessions

Although the approach outlined in this book should enable a class or subject teacher to implement a reading programme, some time will have to be found for individual contact. A private individual session of 15 – 20 minutes once a week is necessary to introduce new work and review progress, and may perhaps be fitted in during a lunchtime or non-teaching period. It should be an opportunity for the pupil to reflect and comment on his remedial programme and participate in the decision making, rather than just an occasion for the teacher to tell him what to do next. The activities for the week can be planned but how much time can be offered beyond this 15 – 20 minute session, and how the pupil's reading activities are organised throughout the week, will of course vary according to the teacher's workload and the child's timetable. Several other short periods will be needed when the pupil can complete different reading tasks — as far as possible activities that do not demand the teacher's attention and can be undertaken during normal class lesson time.

During the individual session start by explaining to the pupil the objectives to be worked on and introduce any new words. For example, if one objective for that week is that the pupil should be able to read the words 'I go shopping on Saturday with my Mum' (or 'I go to football on Saturday with my Dad') both in the context of the sentence and individually, you could begin by reading the complete sentence to the pupil, then let him repeat it while you point to the words, drawing attention to any capital letters, length of the words, or similarities with other words he has learnt, and so on, making sure also that if illustrations are used they are easily identifiable.

The constraints of the timetable may mean that you have no choice about the lessons during which reading activities should take place, but it is worth thinking carefully about the times of the day when the pupil is most likely to learn. You should also bear in mind the lesson which has immediately preceded your proposed reading session; pupils returning from swimming or games, for example, will take time to settle and concentrate.

For the majority of children frequent short sessions will be best. For those at the very early stages of learning to read with a long history of failure, begin with as little as ten minutes reading activity a day and gradually increase this as they become more competent. You will find that establishing routines for seating position and times of reading sessions is useful too. Even if the need for your individual help is kept to a minimum, some classroom routines and rules about who gets your attention when, will help you to see that no individual or group is neglected. In a mixed ability class it is possible to set aside certain periods for reading work with your poor readers by dividing the class into groups and specifying the times when you will attend to each group. If you have three groups — Red, Blue and Green — the class may be told that for the next twenty minutes you will be giving help only to Blue group and not helping or dealing with queries from Red and Green groups. The groups then rotate so that each has its share of your attention. As long as pupils know that they will eventually have your attention, have been given clear guidelines about what they should do if they are genuinely unable to continue without assistance, and you show that you are still supervising the whole class, then this arrangement can work very well. It is probably easier to organise if the groups working alone are able to check their own work, as they would if working from one of the reading laboratories or workshops (e.g. SRA, Ward Lock, Longman Reading Routes). Many of the teacher-produced class tasks described later can be made self-correcting.

Presentation

Detailed suggestions for activities and materials take up the major part of this chapter, but a few general points about presentation need to be made first. It is important that the pupil should be able to complete successfully all the tasks he is given. Obviously, it is better if he can do this without coming out for help. The task must therefore be at the right level for the pupil and all the necessary cues provided in the material. In the early stages of learning new words, the material may have picture cues which make it impossible for the pupil to fail the task. The picture cues may gradually be removed and the tasks made more difficult until he is able to read the words without assistance. The use of a reference card, listing the words to be learnt, each with a picture or illustration to indicate the meaning, is one way of providing cues. Initially the pupil can keep the card on his desk so that he can make constant reference to it, but then when he has begun to learn some of the words the card may be kept inside his desk or bag and used only when his memory fails or to check completed work. Finally, the card may be left on the other side of the room or in the teacher's possession. This gradually increases the effort the pupil must make to use the card as a prop, and encourages independence from it whilst allowing the pupil the reassurance that he can always use it to check a word if necessary. It can also save him the embarrassment of having to ask the teacher if he is unsure of something, avoid repetition of errors and give the pupil greater responsibility for his own learning.

The materials used, whether purchased or made, particularly those with illustrations, should be attractive and appropriate to the age of the pupil, but should also draw attention to the relevant information and not detract from it by being over-embellished. Some published materials, designed to appeal to teenage tastes, are full of colour and detail and, although they may be attractive to young people, there is so much to catch the attention that it is not easy to grasp immediately what is relevant to the task in hand.

Marking Success

A child who has not experienced much success before may not recognise it when it comes, nor find it intrinsically rewarding. The teacher's role after the pupil has completed a task is therefore as important in marking and rewarding the child's successes as in the careful preparation and selection of material.

Signalling the pupil's achievements, giving feedback or knowledge of results, is all part of the general approach to pupil involvement. If he has been checking his own work (as he might with a reference card), then the teacher's role is largely one of helping the pupil to recognise the purpose of the tasks and whether and how the purpose has been achieved. Pupils can be helped to reflect on their successful learning strategies. For example, what features of the words

Figure 5: Two Record Charts

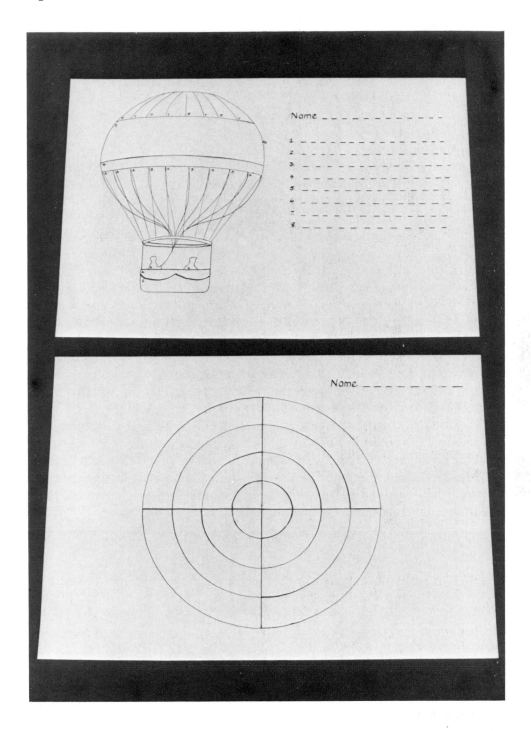

did the pupil attend to help him remember them? Does a mnemonic help him to recall which way 'b' and 'd' face? For many pupils just the knowledge of success will be sufficient, others may need something more tangible. The pupil, as well as the teacher, can keep a record of mastered objectives, so that he has tangible evidence of his previous achievements. Older pupils can use a record form identical to that of the teacher (see p. 29), but for younger pupils some other form of progress chart, perhaps in the form of a picture, is more suitable (see Figure 5 for two such examples). The picture was designed for 11 – 12 year-olds, the target for 13 – 14 year old pupils. Objectives may either be written in the segments or listed separately.

For some pupils success alone, or success combined with social rewards (like praise) will not be sufficient and additional rewards will have to be considered. Activity rewards are the most readily available form of reinforcement in the classroom. The pupil who has completed a task or mastered an objective is allowed to engage in an activity he enjoys (e.g. drawing) for a set period of time. It is usually possible to find several activities a pupil enjoys, perhaps including 'jobs' or errands such as taking the register or tidying books, in which case a list may be prepared from which the child may choose. Some teachers may like to use some of the games described later in this section in this way, as a reward for less appealing work. Whatever rewards you use should always be accompanied by social praise as one would hope that social reward alone will eventually be sufficient. A massive incentive in the form of a highly desirable reward should not be offered for successful attainment of a goal if that goal is too difficult or patently beyond the pupil's reach. It will simply cause frustration and may well lead to the pupil opting out completely. I have known well-intentioned parents who have promised their son or daughter a bicycle if they can learn to read by the end of the term, the equivalent of which would probably be someone offering you a trip round the world if you could learn to speak fluent Chinese within the next three months! It is worth making sure that parents do not have unrealistic expectations, especially if they learn that their son or daughter is following a special remedial programme.

Some Activities and Materials for Teaching a Sight Vocabulary

Teacher Produced Material

The materials and activities described here have all been found useful in the teaching of a sight vocabulary to pupils of various ages. They will not all be useful to every child, and you will want to choose those that are appropriate to your objectives. There should be a sufficient variety of tasks to cater for those children who need to learn in very small steps, and who need considerable repetition. The tasks are roughly graded with the simpler tasks, where many picture cues are provided, coming at the beginning. How many cues are needed, and how they are graded, will of course depend on the individual, and this can only be discovered in the process of removing these learning props through an experimental approach to teaching. The use of the reference card (item (1)) has already been discussed; its advantages are that the pupil has some control over its use, and that it can easily be re-introduced if he seems to need further support. There are also pupils who initially will need picture cues on the card or worksheet they are using rather than on a separate card.

The suggestions listed require little in the way of raw materials; most can be made with white card, paper, glue and felt tips. Materials last better and perhaps look more attractive if covered in adhesive plastic film, but this is time-consuming and can be quite expensive. White workcards with a wipe-over surface can be purchased from W.F. Tyson & Sons, Nottingham. Spirit-based fibre tip ink passes through the surface which can then be wiped clean of grubby finger marks with a damp cloth, leaving the writing or drawing intact.

Although care is required in the preparation of the materials, it is not necessary to be an artist. If you can draw and enjoy drawing, fine, if not, make use of magazine and comic illustrations, cutting them out to use or tracing them. If someone from the art department is prepared to help, ask them to produce a few relevant drawings and then reproduce them for your workcards and sheets by tracing or duplicating them from a spirit master.

(1) *Reference Card.* It may be necessary to find illustrations for words other than common nouns, e.g. action verbs, prepositions, in which case you will need to be sure that the pupil understands and remembers the meaning of the illustration.

(2) *Sentence Matching With Picture Cues.* The pupil is simply required to match the sentences. The picture reminds him of the meaning of the sentence. With this task, and many that follow, the pupil may be asked to write the sentences once the matching is complete. It is obviously helpful if at some point the pupil can read the sentences to someone. If the pupil finds card matching a 'babyish' activity, a worksheet can be made instead.

(3) *Matching Words to Sentences With Picture Cues.*

(4) *Sentence Matching Without Pictures.*

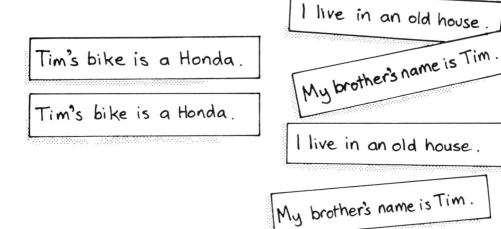

(5) *Matching Words to Sentences Without Pictures.*

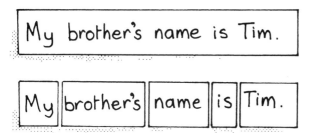

(6) *Matching Sentences or Phrases to Pictures.*

(7) *Matching Words to Pictures.* This is of course restricted to words that can be illustrated.

(8) *Word Matching With Visually Distinct Alternatives.*

(9) *Word Matching With Visually Similar Alternatives.*

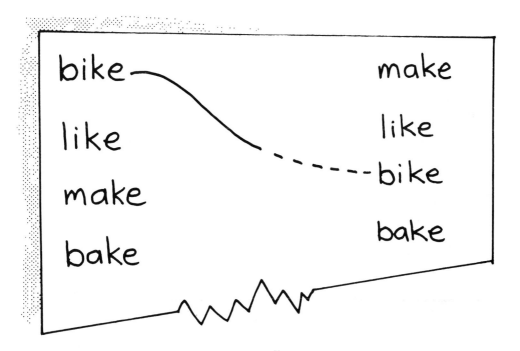

(10) *Sentence Puzzles (i).* Sentences are written on strips of card and cut into two or three pieces with jagged edges. The pupil may copy the sentences once they are correctly assembled and illustrate them if he chooses.

(11) *Sentence Puzzles (ii).* The sentences are written on strips of card as above, but are this time cut with straight edges to remove the extra cues.

Tim was | on his bike.

(12) *Word puzzles (i).* These are like the sentence puzzles described above, but this time words are cut into pieces.

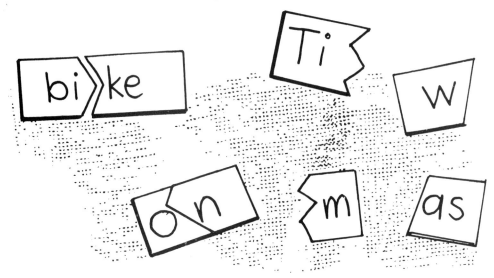

(13) *Word Puzzles (ii).*

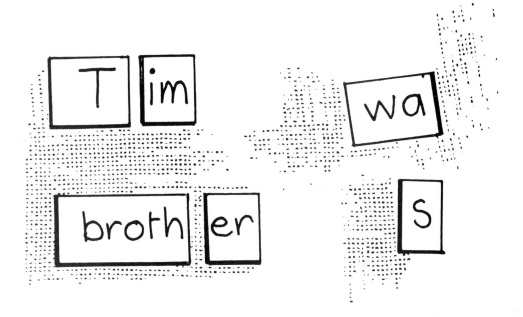

(14) *Missing Word Cards.* The pupil copies the passage or sentences inserting the missing words. A selection of words from which to choose may be written at the bottom of the card or, if the vocabulary is based on a reading book, the pupil may use the book for reference.

I ____ to the shops on Saturday. I do the ____ for my Mum. I like going to the bakers best because I choose ____ cakes.

(15) *Missing Letter Cards.* These are similar to (14) but with letters deleted instead of words. This is one of the tasks for which a reference card may be used if necessary.

I go to t_e shops on Saturday . I do the shopping _or my Mu_. I l_ke goi_g to the bakers

(16) *'Make a Picture' Cards*. These are cards on which a passage or a few sentences are written. The pupil reads the card and draws a picture illustrating all the detail given in the passage. If you are using a reading series, particularly if you are using it with more than one pupil, you may like to produce a set of illustrations of the characters and objects in the series, mount these on card, and then attach felt or magnets so that they can be used on a feltboard or metal board. Pupils who are reluctant to draw may enjoy assembling scenes with these as an alternative, although with secondary-age children, one must take care to ensure that this does not look like infant or junior material.

(17) *Question Cards*. These are cards with a picture or a passage and a series of related questions. It is a good idea to begin with questions that require simply a *yes* or *no* answer.

(18) *Instruction Cards*. This suggestion is probably most useful for subject teachers. The pupil is given a series of instructions which he must read and then carry out (e.g. 'Look at the map of France on page – – . Write in your book the names of all the towns on the coast.'). Any activity which requires the pupil to do something after reading a sentence or passage is desirable as it gives purpose to the reading activity and ensures that the pupil is reading for meaning.

(19) *Disordered Passages*. A passage is written on card and then cut into sections. The pupil re-arranges the jumbled sections so that the passage makes sense. He may then write out the passage or, if the subject is a practical one, carry out the instructions.

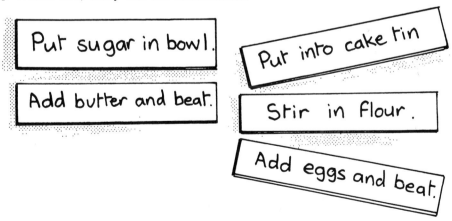

You may, for example, put the instructions for a science experiment or a simple recipe on pieces of card, then ask the pupil to put them in order and write the sentences in his book. This activity can follow on from a practical demonstration or be a preparation for the next lesson.

Stories. This activity is really only suitable for pupils who ͻ. A child may be asked to design his own comic strip from ͻ he has learnt, or be given the captions and asked to illus-

(21) *Passages with Deleted Words.* These are slightly different from the missing word cards described earlier. The pupil is given a passage with every tenth word deleted. He reads the passage and guesses the missing words. He is not offered any alternatives from which to choose as there are no strict right and wrong answers: any word which makes sense is acceptable. If the pupil reads the passage into a tape recorder he is free to use words he cannot write.

(22) *Word Snap.* Snap games are simple to organise and usually greatly enjoyed. A pack of flashcards with two cards of each word is all that is required. Ordinary workcards can be used, but Waddingtons produce blank playing cards for this purpose which are much nicer to handle.

(23) *Dominoes.* The dominoes game can be adapted as another word-picture matching activity. To make the dominoes work card may be cut into rectangles (approx. 8cm x 4cm) or the Waddingtons blank playing cards can be used. A line is drawn down the centre to divide the card into two squares and a word or picture drawn at each end. Each word needs to be represented (by picture or in writing) an even number of times to allow for matching.

The cards are shared between two or more people who then take turns in laying cards to match those already placed. The first person to lay all his cards is the winner.

(24) *Pokey.* A series of holes, of slightly larger diameter than a pencil, are cut in a sheet of card. On one side of the card, just below each hole, a word is written, and on the other side of the card a corresponding picture is drawn below each hole.

One pupil sits holding the card with the picture side towards him and asks another pupil, who is looking at the words, to push his pencil through the appropriate hole as he says each word.

(25) *Word bingo.* A well-known game which is a useful idea for a group of poor readers. Each pupil has a 'bingo' card with the words written on, while the teacher has a pile of individual word cards. The teacher picks out

	house	name	
is	Tim		our
	street	bike	
my		live	brother

and reads cards from the pile, and the pupil covers the word (or crosses it out) if it is on his card. The first to cover all his words is the winner. The pupils playing the game will probably each be working on a different set of words, in which case each pupil has a bingo card covering just the words he is learning.

The game can be varied by using ESA First Words Cards (p. 54) with the teacher showing the *photograph* while the pupils identify the corresponding words on their card.

(26) *Fishing game.* This is only suitable for younger pupils. Words are written inside fish-shaped folded cards which are held closed with a paper clip. These are placed in a box and players take turns in 'fishing' for words. The player keeps the fish if he can read the word and the winner is the player with the most fish at the end of the game. Some children enjoy making the fish and choosing the words to write in more than actually playing the game!

(27) *Board Games.* A wide range of board games can be devised based on the idea of a track with 'target' squares at intervals along the track. A player landing on a red square, for example, may have to take and read a card from the red pack. Sentences and instructions can be included in the pack cards as well as individual words.

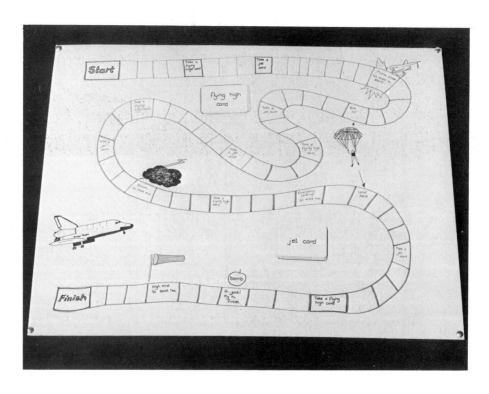

(28) *Snakes and Ladders.* An ordinary snakes and ladders board can be adapted to make a word game. Words are written at the bottom of the ladders and at the top of the snakes. A player landing at the bottom of a ladder may only move his counter up if he can read the word at the bottom, and a player landing at the top of a snake can *avoid* having to go down by reading the word placed at the top of the snake. Placing the easier words at the top of the snakes and the harder ones at the bottom of ladders avoids too many frustrations. If you cover the board with plastic film and attach adhesive labels for the words, the words can be peeled off and changed when necessary.

Published Materials for Teaching a Sight Vocabulary

There are, in fact, very few published materials of value in teaching a basic sight vocabulary to older pupils. Carefully graded reading schemes with supplementary material are not available for secondary-age pupils as they are for primary school children. It would, of course, be quite difficult to produce such material as it would need to be suitable for children of different ages with a variety of interests. As discussed in the section on programme planning, the words one chooses to include in a sight vocabulary, especially in the very early stages, need to be specially produced anyway. It can, however, be useful to include the vocabulary of a particular book or series of books in the words you are teaching by sight. Any book(s) you use for this purpose must be fairly short, and have a controlled vocabulary and relatively simple sentence structure. The following are worth considering for pupils who know only a few words as long as supplementary material is prepared, and the pupil learns the vocabulary *before* he is presented with the book to read.

Carford Readers. Evan Owen. (Pergamon Press)
A series of eight books about a group of children living in a town called Carford. The vocabulary is controlled and one could easily produce line drawings based on the illustrations for supplementary material. It is a good starting point for pupils with little or no sight vocabulary as the first book contains fewer than 50 different words, but the series is likely to appeal only to younger secondary pupils.

Look-out Gang. M. B. Chaplin. (Robert Gibson & Sons)
A series of six books about a group of children who form a gang to watch for criminals — implausible adventure story stuff but with an appeal to some children. The vocabulary is well controlled and the new words for each page are listed at the back. Many of the words are phonically regular, but teaching them as sight words at this stage can help in later teaching of phonic skills.

ESA First Words Cards.
Also useful for many games to teach a basic sight vocabulary are these photographs of 110 everyday objects (words on the back). Although black and white they are very popular with pupils of all ages and can be used for self-testing or in pairs, or by a teacher with a group. Some of the words are easy to read, to give confidence (e.g. pen, tree), others more demanding (e.g. scissors, biscuit).

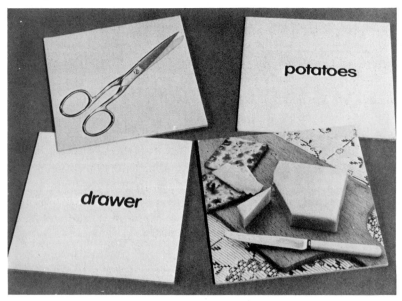

Activities and Materials for Teaching Phonics

It is easier to find commercial materials for teaching phonics to secondary pupils than it is to find sight vocabulary material, but you will probably still need to make some things yourself, either because the published material does not quite fit your programme, or because it is too expensive.

Teacher Produced Material

Although many of the activities and materials described here can be adapted for different stages of phonic teaching, some are specific to a particular stage. The activities are listed with those suitable for teaching initial letter sounds coming first, progressing to materials for 3-letter blends and more difficult sounds, reflecting the order given for phonic teaching in Chapter 2. The tasks can be adapted to suit your objectives.

Discriminating Initial Letter Sounds:

(1) *Identifying Whether Words Begin With the Same or Different Sounds.* Pairs of words are read into a tape recorder and the child records for each pair whether the initial sound was the same or different. A tape recorder with headphones is extremely useful, but should a recorder not be available then the teacher or another pupil may simply read the words aloud.

(2) *Grouping Pictures of Nouns According to Initial Letter Sound.* Make a collection of picture cards by drawing objects or cutting pictures from magazines (mail order catalogues are a good source). The pupil then sorts the pictures into groups according to the initial letter sound. Make sure you agree on the name for an object before you begin. If you build up a good collection of picture cards they can also be used for later phonic activities.

(3) *Picture Snap.* The cards produced for the activity above can be used to play a game where pictures of objects beginning with the same initial *sound* are 'snapped' (note that 'sausages' could be snapped with 'celery').

(4) *I Spy.* Younger secondary school children, especially those in lower ability groups, can still enjoy this game, which should be played with the letter *sounds*, not their names.

(5) *Picture Worksheets.* The pupil draws a line joining pictures of objects which begin with the same letter sound.

Discriminating Initial Letter Symbols:

(6) *Letter Matching Worksheets.* It is helpful to draw the pupil's attention to the salient differences, e.g. which side the stick is on or whether the curved line is at the top or the bottom of the letter.

Associating Initial Letter Sounds and Symbols:

(7) *Reference Card (Sounds).* A reference card giving picture clues for the sound of each letter is useful. It may be used in the same way as the sight vocabulary reference card (see p. 41). Pictures can be drawn to indicate the shape of the letter. Those shown here were devised by Angela White of the Leicestershire Reading Service. Other examples can be found in *Reading and Reading Failures* by John Hughes (Evans Brothers Ltd, London, 1975).

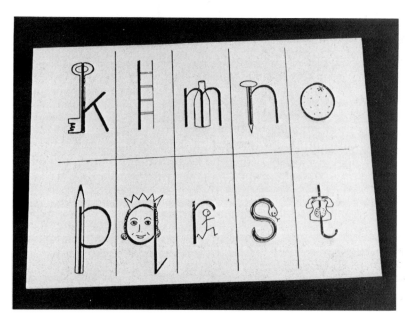

(8) *Picture-letter Worksheets or Workcards.* These may be made as expendable worksheets or as workcards to be used with a laminate sheet and felt tip pen. Four examples are shown here but many variations on the same theme can be produced.

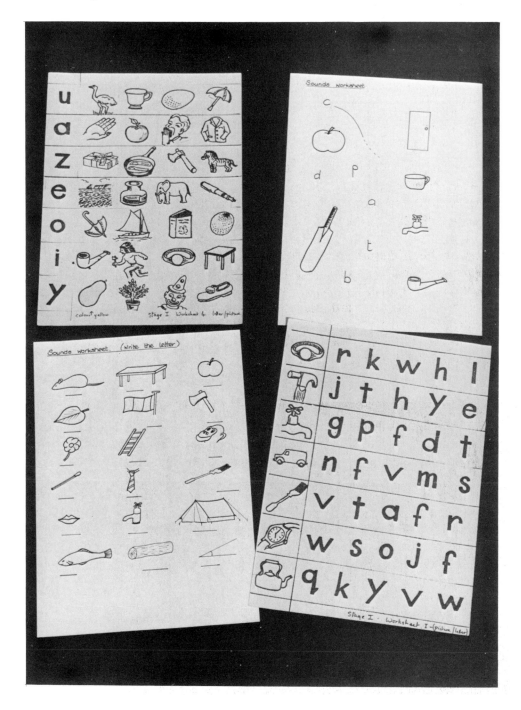

(9) *Mixed Dominoes.* The cards have a picture at one end and a letter at the other. Players may match a picture to its initial letter, a picture to another picture with the same initial sound, or letter to letter. The winner is the first person to lay all his cards.

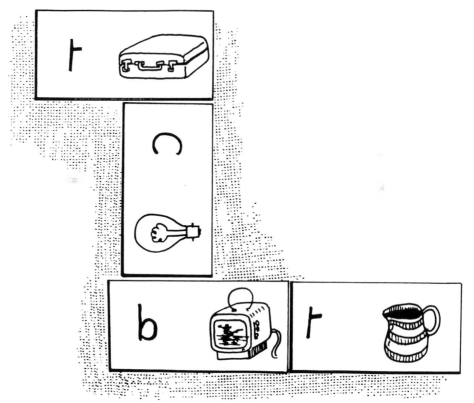

(10) *Mixed Snap.* The picture cards from activity (3) can be used and a pack of letter cards added. Players may snap pictures with the same initial letter sound, a letter and a picture that begins with that sound, or identical letters.

(11) *Pelmanism.* The cards from the snap game are used. They are spread, face down, on the table and players take turns to turn over two cards. The aim is to find a pair representing the same sound which may be two picture cards, two letter cards, or a letter card and a picture card. A player who turns over a matching pair keeps those two cards and has a second turn. The winner is the player with the most pairs when all the cards have been won. In order to win, players must pay attention to, and remember, the cards turned up by other players and their positions on the table.

(12) *Letter Flash Cards.* This is something the well-motivated pupil can do alone or with a parent or brother or sister. The letter cards from (10) and

(11) above are used. The pupil simply goes thro
either the letter sound, or a word beginning with
go through the cards more and more quickly until
soon as he sees the letter.

Reading Phonetically Regular Words of Three Letters or

(13) *Reference Sounds Book*. The pupil keeps an exercise
writes each new sound or word family he learns. Each
word at the top, with the important sound underlined or w
and an illustration. The pupil adds words that belong to t.   ...y as he
comes across them.

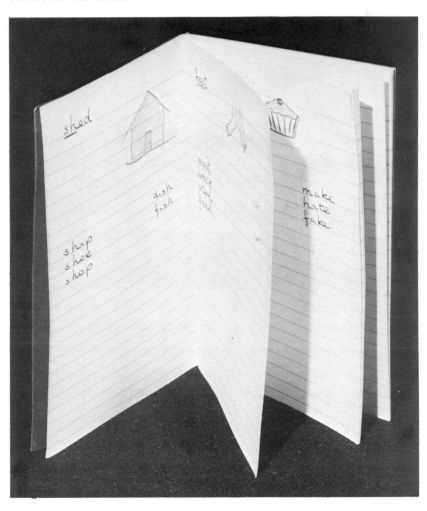

(14) *Chain Games*. These are suitable for younger pupils. Draw a long picture
of a snake, train or traffic jam, mount on a card and cut into sections.

Write words on the sections with the beginning of the word on the end of one card and the end of the word on the beginning of another card.

The cards are shared between two or more players. The player with the head of the snake or the engine of the train begins and then players take turns in laying cards to build words, reading each word they make, until one player has laid all his cards. The player who has the tail of the picture must lay it as the last of his cards. For older pupils the words may be written on plain cards and the pictures omitted.

The game illustrated was made from a sheet produced at the Lansdowne House Teachers' Centre, Leicester.

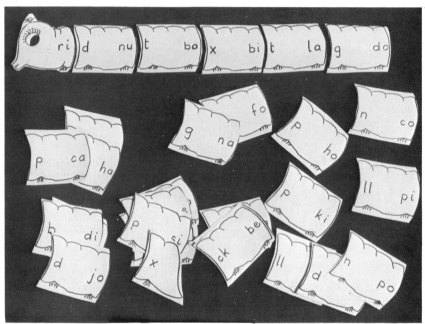

(15) *Missing Letter Cards.*

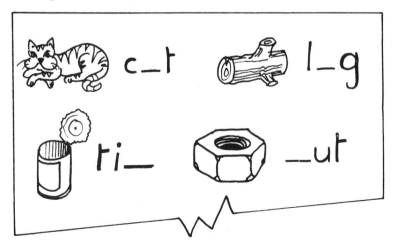

(16) *Picture-word Matching.* Cards or worksheets can be used here (as described for item (7) of the sight vocabulary activities but with phonically regular words).

(17) *Missing Word Worksheets or Workcards.*

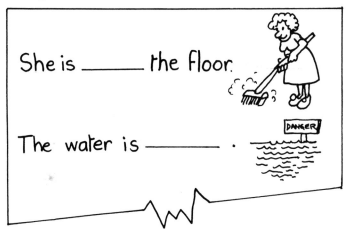

She is ——— the floor.

The water is ——— .

(18) *Word Wheels.* Cut two circles from stiff card, one of them 14cm diameter and one 8cm diameter. Fit them together through their centres with a tack type paper clip so that the smaller one rotates on the larger one. Initial letters or initial blends are written on the edge of the larger circle and word endings on the smaller circle. The pupil rotates the discs to make words which he then writes in his notebook.

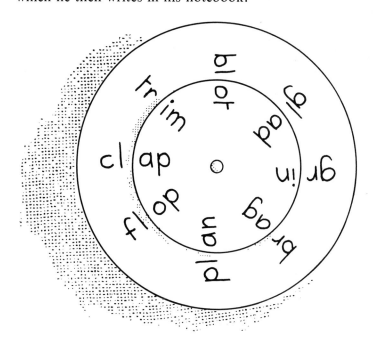

(19) *Word Builders*. A rectangular piece of stiff card has slits cut in it to take
long thin strips of more pliable card. Letters are written on the strips and
on the main card so that as the long strip is pulled, different letters appear
in the 'window' of the main card producing different words. You may
begin with a simple version with one strip and progress to one with several
strips where all the letters may be changed.

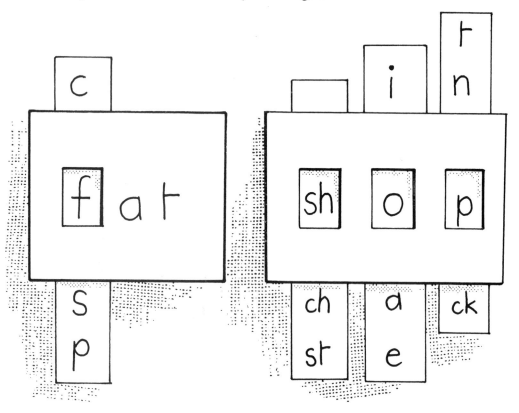

(20) *Flash Cards*. It can be very useful for the pupil to carry a set of flash cards
of the words he is learning. He should be encouraged to look at them
himself whenever he has a spare few minutes to see how many he can
remember, and encouraged to read them at least once a day to a
sympathetic teacher/parent/brother/sister/friend.

(21) *Word Families (i)*. You will need 20 blank cards (the Waddington blank
playing cards are ideal). Four of the cards are made into 'master sounds
cards' on which there is a clue word with a picture, and four other words
containing the same sound. On the remaining cards draw or stick pictures
to represent the 16 unillustrated words from the master cards. Each player
takes a master sound card and the other cards are dealt. The aim is for
each player to collect all the picture cards that go with the words on his
master card. Turns are taken in asking one of the other players 'Do you

have the picture of the − − −?' as in Happy Families. The winner is the first player to collect his 'sound family'.

4 master cards.

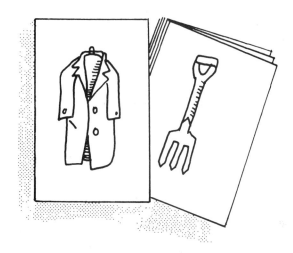

16 picture cards

(22) *Word families (ii).* Make a long illustrated master card with two or more sounds represented, and a pack of flashcards with several words for each of the families represented on the master card. The master card is placed on the table with the pack beside it. Players take a card from the pack, hold it next to the appropriate word on the master card and read aloud *both* words. If the pupil reads the words correctly he keeps the card, but if he does not it is replaced at the bottom of the pack. To avoid the need for a teacher to act as arbiter for disputed words, picture clues may be drawn on the reverse of the word cards, or a reference card consulted.

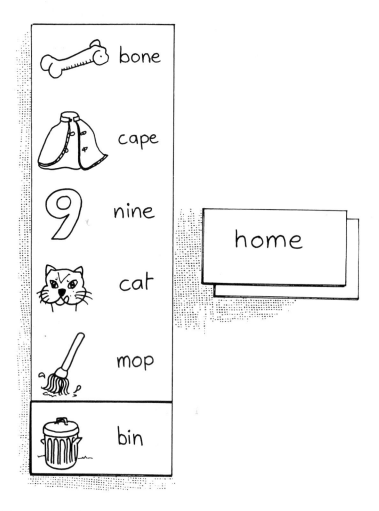

When a pupil becomes more confident with phonic blends then activities can be devised combining the words in his sight vocabulary with the phonetically regular words he is learning, for example, passages with deleted words, games like Junior Scrabble, and so on.

Published Materials for Teaching Phonics

There is a good range of material designed to help teach phonic word attack which can be used successfully with secondary age pupils. The problem is in knowing what materials to choose and how to use them. This section gives some guidance but you will need to select on the basis of the age and interests of your pupils, and on the content of your reading programme(s). One thing to bear in mind is what materials your pupils have encountered in their primary schools. Some may like to continue with familiar materials, at least at first: others prefer

to avoid books associated with junior school and past failures, and make a fresh start. The materials listed here, which are felt to be the more useful ones, do vary considerably in price from the cheap Ginn Phonic Workbooks to the fairly expensive Stott Programmed Reading Kit. All, however, are value for money, *if they meet the needs of your pupils.* If you have chosen a workbook because it covers several of the sounds you will be teaching, for example, do not just give it to a pupil to work straight through as it may not cover the sounds in the order you have chosen, and it is unlikely to be at just the right pace. If it moves too quickly the pupil will learn little and become muddled; if it moves too slowly he will be wasting time and become bored. Either way your careful planning of objectives will be defeated. There is a temptation to occupy poor readers with workbooks because they are often limited in the extent to which they can complete the work set the rest of the class. If it is necessary simply 'to occupy' a child, accept that that is what you are doing and do not waste your valuable reading materials.

The National Association of Remedial Education publishes a book which shows just what material covers which sounds. If you look up a particular sound there is a list of appropriate material with the page numbers given where relevant. *A Classroom Index of Phonic Resources*, compiled by Doris Herbert and Gareth Davies-Jones, is available from NARE Central Office, 4 Oldcroft Road, Walton-on-the-Hill, Stafford, ST17 0LF.

Workbooks and Worksheets.
(1) *Booster Workbooks.* W. C. H. Chalk. (Heinemann Educational)
   A series of five re-usable workbooks.

(2) *Domain Phonic Workshop.* J. McLeod and J. Atkinson. (Oliver & Boyd)
   34 inexpensive double-sided worksheets providing a number of exercises for each group of sounds.

(3) *Ginn Phonic Workbooks.* E. S. Grassam. (Ginn)
   A series of six expendable workbooks, beginning with initial letter sounds in the first workbook and covering single syllable words with vowel digraphs by Book 6. The first two books are particularly useful in providing plenty of exercises at the initial letter stage, although you may want to omit some of the pages on blending two or three sounds which seem misplaced. Pupils are unlikely to be able to read the instructions at the top of each page, but this need not be a problem where you are presenting just a few pages at a time. On a number of pages the activities include colouring the pictures, which can be ignored, of course, if it seems inappropriate.

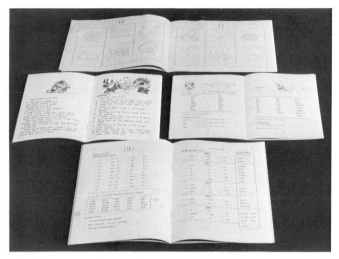

(4) *Moving on with Reading.* John Hughes. (Collins)
A series of three workbooks which need not be written in by the pupil.

(5) *Oxford Senior Worksheets.* Stephen Jackson. (Oxford University Press)
A set of four books of spirit masters. These sheets are intended 'to assist in teaching fundamental reading skills', but also 'to stimulate the reluctant reader and writer to respond to what he sees and hears about him', and thus only about a quarter of the pages deal specifically with phonic skills. The informal and lively but very clear layout of the sheets appeals to pupils, and you may find that sheets other than the phonic ones can be integrated into your programme.

(6) *Sounds Pictures and Words.* John Hughes. (Nelson)
The illustrations and style of presentation may be rather young for some pupils. As the sounds are sometimes presented in isolation you will have to ensure that plenty of other material giving whole words in context is used.

(7) *Sound Sense.* A. E. Tansley. (E.J. Arnold)
A set of eight workbooks (not written in by the pupil). These are very popular books of phonic exercises in common use in both primary and secondary schools. Surprisingly, many secondary age pupils do not find the illustrations 'babyish'. There is an emphasis on the meaning of words individually and in sentences and passages.

(8) *Sounds and Words.* Southgate and Havenhand. (Hodder & Stoughton)
A set of six re-usable workbooks. These are basically books of useful lists of phonically regular words with one or two exercises at the bottom of each page.

(9) *Wordslides.* Frederick Caudle. (Longman)

Six graded packs of workcards (which can be bought separately). Level 1 is concerned with visual discrimination, and initial letter sounds begin at level 2. They are called Wordslides because a strip of card is pulled out from the bottom of the workcard to reveal the answers. This built-in self-checking device, plus the fact that a pack can be shared by several pupils, make them a useful classroom resource.

Games

(10) *Programmed Reading Kit.* D. H. Stott. (Holmes MacDougall)

This is a kit of 29 carefully graded activities including games and workcards. Although more expensive than much of the material listed, it provides a wide range of well planned teaching and consolidation activities.

(11) *Betty Root Reading Games.* Betty Root. (Rupert Hart-Davies)

These are boxes of small cards to be used for pelmanism type games. One box contains letter cards intended for making words which may also be useful in teaching initial letter sounds.

(12) *Good Reading Games.* (Good Reading Ltd)

A range of board games which includes some phonic ones. The games in the Take One series are useful for teaching initial consonant blends and word endings.

(13) *Royal Road Reading Apparatus.* Daniels and Diack. (Philip & Tacey)

A series of word games in small plastic boxes. The missing letter games where either initial, final or medial sound has to inserted, are especially good.

Books. These are phonetically based readers which give pupils an opportunity to use their phonic word attack skills in reading stories. They include irregular words as well as phonetically regular ones, so you will need to ensure that the majority of these are in the pupil's vocabulary.

(14) *Bangers and Mash.* Paul Groves. (Longman)
A series of 14 books of silly stories about two chimps called Bangers and Mash. Each book concentrates on a particular sound or set of sounds, which leads to some rather contrived language, although this does not prevent their being enjoyed enormously by some children.

(15) *Look-out Gang.* M. B. Chaplin. (Robert Gibson & Sons)
Already recommended in an earlier section, the books include common sight words as well as the phonetically regular ones. The vocabulary is well controlled and new words for each page are helpfully listed at the back.

(16) *Sound Sense Supplementary Readers.* A. E. Tansley. (E.J. Arnold)
A series of readers for use alongside the Sound Sense exercise books.

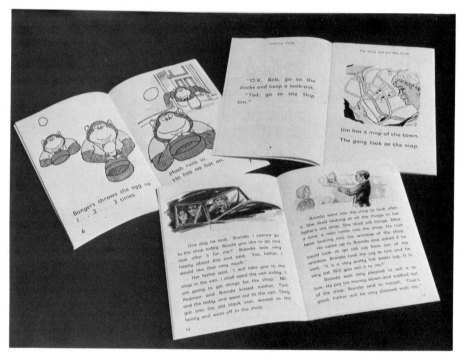

None of the materials or the ideas for producing material listed in this section is new and many will be already familiar to teachers. The purpose in listing them together in this way is to make readily available a variety of activities for use in teaching to your objectives. Their success depends upon their being used as part of a programme designed to meet the pupil's learning needs.

APPENDIX A

Reading Tests Suitable for Secondary Age Pupils

The tests listed here are ones which can be used with secondary age pupils to give an indication of their reading levels. The group tests are suitable for screening large numbers of pupils to identify those having reading difficulties when this information is not already available. Most of the tests here cover a wide age range, which, while making them useful for screening purposes, does, for the shorter tests especially, limit reliability. Caution is therefore needed in quoting scores and interpreting differences between scores (see p. 2).

Individual Tests

Title	Author	Publisher	Age Range
Burt (re-arranged) Word Reading Test (1938)	C. Burt revised by P. E. Vernon	now out of print	5.0 – 14.0
Burt Word Reading Test, 1974 Revision	C. Burt revised by Scottish Council for Research in Education	Hodder & Stoughton Educational	

This is an individual word recognition test used fairly widely in both primary and secondary schools. In 1972 Shearer produced new norms for the 1938 test based on a sample of 6,000 5 – 11 year olds.

The 1974 revision, which supersedes all previous versions of the test, was standardised on a sample of 2,200 Scottish primary school children.

Neale Analysis of Reading Ability	M. D. Neale	Macmillan	6.0 – 12.0

This is an individual test with three parallel forms. The test consists of six prose passages of increasing length and complexity. The pupil reads the passages aloud and then answers questions on the content. Norms are given for reading accuracy, speed and comprehension.

Schonell Graded Word Reading Test	F. Schonell	Oliver & Boyd	5.0 – 15.0

This is another commonly used individual word recognition test. New norms based on a sample of 10,000 Salford school children aged 6.9 – 11.9 were issued in 1972. Shearer restandardised the test on 6,000 6 – 11 year olds in Cheshire.

Group Tests

Title	Author	Publisher	Age Range
GAPADOL Reading Comprehension Test	J. McLeod and J. Anderson	Heinemann Educational	7.3 – 16.11

This is a group test with two parallel forms, which is relatively easy to administer and mark. Pupils are required to read silently six prose passages inserting omitted words. Acceptable responses are only those given in the manual but spelling errors are not penalised. The standardisation information given in the manual is limited, but standard errors are provided. These should be taken into account when quoting scores.

SPAR Reading Test	D. Young	Hodder & Stoughton Educational	7.0 – 15.11

This is a group test consisting of picture-word matching and sentence completion items, which has been standardised on 3,797 primary and 936 secondary pupils.

Wide Span Reading Test	M. A. Brimer and H. Gross	Nelson	7.0 – 15.0

This is a group test of multiple choice sentence completion items, with the advantage of a re-usable test booklet. Test-retest reliability is given, based on a sample of children claimed to be representative of the national distribution.

Graded Test of Reading Experience	J. C. Daniels and Hunter Diack	Chatto & Windus	6.0 – 14 +

This group test is included in the authors' *Standard Reading Tests* (1958) and can be typed and stencilled or photocopied. It does not discriminate very well beyond the 9½ year level (too few test items).

APPENDIX B

Reading Series Suitable for Secondary Age Pupils

The following is a selective list of books suitable for secondary age poor readers, with a guide to reading and interest levels. A more comprehensive list will be found in *An A to Z of Reading and Subject Books* by Atkinson and Gains, obtainable from NARE Central Office.

The reading levels given for the books here should really be taken only as a guide, particularly at the lower reading ages. Whether or not a book is appropriate and at the right reading level will depend on whether the pupil knows most of the words in that particular book, and is motivated to read it. The first book the pupil encounters in the context of your teaching programme should be read with as near to 100 per cent success as possible, so he should learn the vocabulary before being given the book. As he becomes more competent and more confident, he will be able to cope with and tolerate more words that he has to 'guess at' from context — and in this way his sight vocabulary will grow. But it is always advisable to prepare for a new book by teaching the key words. As with all your material, a reading book should never seem so hard to a pupil that he becomes discouraged: remember that the level of difficulty and number of new words that can be coped with depends very much on the pupil's motivation and interest in the material.

Of course, other books from the school or public library should be provided to supplement these 'readers'. Colourful non-fiction publications with a high level of illustration can stimulate pupils to work out the accompanying text even when their reading ability is quite low. Reading should be seen as a pleasurable activity and a useful one for finding things out: hence newspapers and comics should not be disregarded as a source of materials.

Series	Reading Age	Interest Age
Booster Books. W. H. Chalk. (Heinemann) 10 titles. Quite long stories.	8 – 10	11 – 5
Canal Street. M. Durnford. (Nelson) 6 books.	6 – 7	9 – 12
Carford Readers. E. Owen. (Pergamon Press) A series of 8 books.	6 – 8	9 – 13
Cassell Anchor. Various authors. (Cassell) Two sets of 4 books each.	8½ – 9	teens
Cassell Banjo Books. Various authors. (Cassell) Three sets of 4 books each.	7 – 8	teens

Series	Reading Age	Interest Age
Cassell Club. Various authors. (Cassell) Four sets of 4 books each. Stories about teenagers.	6½ – 7½	teens
Cassell Disco. Various authors. (Cassell) 9 books. Very short books with a large number of illustrations.	6+	teens
Checkers. E. Owen. (Evans) 12 titles.	8 – 10	teens
Crown Street Kings. A. Oates. (Macmillan) 18 short books.	7+	11 – 14
First Folk Tales. Mollie Clarke. (Rupert Hart-Davis Educational) Retold folk stories from different countries.	7½ – 8	8 – 13
Flightpath to Reading. S. McCullagh. (E.J. Arnold) Well-told stories about a boy who encounters ghostly figures.	8 – 10	9 – 13
Inner Ring First Red Series. Various authors. (E. Benn)	7 – 8	11 – 13
Inner Ring Second Blue Series. Various authors. (E. Benn)	8 – 9	12 – 14
Inner Ring Third Brown Series. Various authors. (E. Benn)	8 – 9	13 – 16
Inner Ring Sports. R. Kennedy. (E. Benn) 8 titles.	8 – 9	11 – 15
Inner Ring Hipsters. Various authors. (E. Benn) Red Series, 4 titles.	7½ – 8	teens
Green Series, 4 titles.	8 – 8½	teens
Instant Readers. W. H. Chalk. (Heinemann)	5+	teens
Inswingers. R. Ward and G. T. Gregory (Hulton) 6 books about Les who moves from a dead end job to a first division football team. Very readable books with large well-spaced print and photo-style illustrations.	8 – 10	teens
Jim Hunter Books. B. Butterworth and B. Stockdale. (Methuen) 8 titles.	7 – 9	teens
Knockouts. Various authors. (Longman) 24 titles.	7 – 9	teens
Look-out Gang. M. B. Chaplin. (Robert Gibson & Sons) 6 books.	6 – 9	9 – 13
Manxman. C. Edwards. (Dent) 6 titles.	8½	teens
Nippers. Various authors. (Macmillan) Green Series.	7½+	8 – 14
Blue Series.	8+	8 – 14
Oxford Graded Readers. Various authors. (OUP)	8 – 10	8 – 13
Patchwork Paperbacks. Various authors. (Cassell) 12 titles.	7 – 9	9 – 13
Popswingers. R. Ward. (Hulton) 6 books about the rise to fame of a school pop group.	8 – 10	teens
Raft on the River. C. Edwards. (Dent) 6 titles.	6½ – 8	teens
Solos. K. Wood. (Hart-Davis Educational)	7 – 8	teens
Spirals. A. Jackson. (Hutchinson) 16 titles. Supernatural, spy and adventure stories. Intended to be adult in appearance they contain no illustrations. Some of the stories tend to be sensational.	7 – 8	11+

Series	Reading Age	Interest Age
Step up and Read. W. Jones. (University of London Press) 6 titles.	7 +	10 +
Seekers. K. Wood. (Hart-Davis Educational)	7 – 8	teens
Stories for Today. C. Bergman and P. Abbs. (Heinemann) Three sets of 6 books each.	7—9	teens
Teenage Twelve. (Gibson & Sons) 12 phonetically based readers. A little old-fashioned in style and content.	6 – 7	teens
Tempo Books. P. Groves. (Longman) 10 titles.	6 – 7	teens
Trend Approach. Various authors. (Ginn)	6½ – 7	teens
Trend Mainstream. Various authors. (Ginn)	6 – 11	teens
Varieties. J. Tate. (Macmillan)	8 – 11	9 – 13
Rescue Series. P. Scott (Webster)	8 – 9	8 – 13
Rewards Series. J. Webster. (E.J. Arnold)	7 – 9	7 – 13

About the Author

Christine Cassell obtained her first degree in Psychology at Nottingham University, completed her teacher training at Leicester University and went on to teach for three years in the remedial department of a large comprehensive school in Derbyshire. She then spent two years as a peripatetic remedial teacher with Nottinghamshire Schools Psychological Service, teaching groups of poor readers in primary schools, individuals in a 'reading clinic' and running workshops for teachers, whilst studying part-time to obtain a Masters degree in Education. She then returned to Nottingham University to take the MA in Child Development, and now works as an educational psychologist in Leicester.

Acknowledgements

The development of the ideas used in the writing of this book owes a great deal to colleagues in teaching and educational psychology with whom I have worked. I am particularly indebted to Nancy Lane and Gordon Fosterjohn for their help and advice in the teaching of poor readers, and Ena Whittaker for her support in my early years of teaching. I should also like to thank Philip Stringer and Alan Sapsford for their comments on earlier drafts of the manuscript; Paul Livock for the line drawings; Sam Grainger for the photographs (the cover photograph and those on pp. 4 and 37 were taken at Judgemeadow Community College, Leicester); and Bill Gillham for giving me the opportunity to put my ideas into print. Finally, special thanks go to my husband for being an encouraging critic.

C.C.